THE OFFICE COOKBOOK

Also by Jody Cameron Malis
"THE NEWLYWED GAME" COOKBOOK

THE OFFICE
COOKBOOK

by Jody Cameron Malis

TRIDENT PRESS   NEW YORK

SBN: 671–27081–8
LIBRARY OF CONGRESS CATALOG CARD NUMBER: 71–147386

PUBLISHED SIMULTANEOUSLY IN THE UNITED STATES AND CANADA BY TRIDENT
PRESS, A DIVISION OF SIMON & SCHUSTER, INC., 630 FIFTH AVENUE, NEW
YORK, N.Y. 10020

PRINTED IN THE UNITED STATES OF AMERICA

To **H. A.**
whose inspiration made this book possible

1592705

CONTENTS

THE OFFICE
COOKBOOK

1

The Office Cook-in Plan

HOW TO BEAT THE HIGH COST OF EATING LUNCH OUT

The Office Cook-in Revolution is here! It's a quiet, nonviolent, working-girls' revolution against the high cost of eating lunch out. With the prices going up, up, and away and the dollar value going down, down, down, new economical methods are being discovered and practiced successfully every day. Join the Office Cook-in Revolution . . . that's what our book is all about. It's a workable, common-sense solution to help you save money and still enjoy good hot food.

When we compared a luncheon menu that was two years old with a recent one, we were disturbed to learn that the price of the same type of lunch had gone up almost thirty percent. There is no way to beat this inflation spiral. Ordering lunch in doesn't do it; you avoid the waiting for the elevators and the crowds, but the prices and tips still remain high. Coffee wagons that make the rounds in office buildings also have steep prices and limited, not very tasty selections.

Of course, you can bring a sandwich to work . . . but try it for a week or so and you'll find it's a drag! Our bodies and our minds require the stimulation and luxury of a hot, cooked meal. So what's the answer? Girls, the only practical solution to enjoying hot lunches and saving money at the same time is the Office Cook-in Plan. Clear-thinking girls by the thousands are following it right now and proving that the Office Cook-in can be done successfully, with no fuss or muss with meals. And in addition, you will be enjoying hot meals that are more varied and more delicious than those many lunch counters provide.

The Office Cookbook has been written to show you just how to do the whole thing—right on the job. Read on and you will learn about the cooking supplies needed and the techniques involved in preparing fast, tasty, no-bother-to-anyone lunches that you can make using any of the easy-to-do recipes in this book. Now at last you can be free of the lunchtime trauma—the jammed, noisy, assembly-line routine of "eat-it-quick-and-make-room-for-the-next-customer." So start today and join our army of office cooks!

Your Lunch Savings Account

In account with: The Working Girl

Date	With-drawal	Deposit	Interest	Balance
1 year from today	—	$5.00 per week	—	$260.00

The above account can be yours just by following our Office Cook-in Plan.

WHERE THE MONEY GOES

Morning coffee break	$ .40
Lunch plus tip	1.35
Afternoon coffee break	.25
Total	$2.00
Our cost for same	1.00
Total daily savings	$1.00

That's five dollars per week saved. Multiply the five dollars by fifty-two weeks and you've saved 260 dollars for the year! You may even be clever enough to save more while still enjoying the same delicious and healthy meals. Make a list of your daily food-on-the-job expenses, which include lunch, beverages, tips, and any extras. Subtract from the total one dollar, which is the maximum cost for any of the complete lunches and extras in this book. Multiply your balance by five (for days of the week), then by fifty-two (for weeks of the year). Your original total may be higher than our approximate two-dollar listing, but our cost figure remains the same. We have discounted your initial expenses for this project as your bank interest at the end of the year will compensate for the figure spent. Whether you bank your savings or set the money aside for little weekly shopping sprees, you're more ahead than you were before, with just a little effort and no sacrifice. Let's face it. You're not working to pay luncheon checks, so start cooking and save for those extra "goodies" in life.

How to Start the Office Cook-in

We are going to show you how to cook delicious, nutritious, and easy-to-prepare lunches right in your office—meals that will save you at least half of your daily lunch check. That could add up to almost two months' salary by the end of the year. Just think how you could spend all that money—a new wardrobe, a long-dreamed-of vacation, a fatter bank account. Do these thoughts appeal to you? Then read on and become a member of the "Cook-ins."

PLAN YOUR CAMPAIGN

Remember, one universal obstacle will confront you when you attempt to start the cook-in at your office. People always tend to resist something new. Therefore, use diplomacy. Do not march in one day and announce your intentions or demand instant approval from the proper authority.

Step 1: Break the Ice—Casually discuss the high cost of eating out every day. *Win* sympathy for your plight—don't demand it.

Step 2: Introduce the Cook-in Idea—The simplest way to do this is to bring this book to work with you. Pick up some literature on the heat source (gas or electric) available in the office. Clip out some ads that feature the preprocessed foods discussed later in the book (packaged soups, gravy mixes, canned meats, etc.). Keep this literature displayed right near this book and you'll find that co-workers and supervisors will come to know that you're carefully studying the idea of cooking in.

Step 3: Ask Permission to Try It—Before you ask, carefully plan exactly where you want to set up operation. Pick a spot that is out of the way and does not interfere with the flow of work in the office. When you ask for permission suggest the location you've selected and carefully explain that the materials you will bring in won't take up more space than an average shoe box. Your heat source, whether it be gas (butane burner) or electric (skillet), can easily be stored in a desk or file drawer.

You've asked for cooking privileges courteously, sensibly, and with a simple but complete explanation of the whole procedure, emphasizing that there will be no fuss or disruption of the office routine. Permission granted! Now you're on your way to big savings and a new enjoyment of lunchtime. But please remember these four rules so that your cooking privileges will never be taken away:

1. Be extremely neat before, during, and after each meal.
2. Never create a fuss over your doings involving co-workers.
3. Avoid heavy cooking odors.
4. Show your appreciation for this privilege by being a cheerful, efficient worker!

Necessary Equipment

Remember that the theme of this program is to save money and enjoy delicious, satisfying, favorite meals with the least amount of effort and little or no cleanup. As delighted as you may be with the idea of the Office Cook-in, bear in mind that you are going to set up housekeeping in the office.

Listed below is the equipment you will need. You may want to add to the list as you go along. Purchase these items at the supermarket or local variety store for additional savings. Fancy paper plates, napkins, mats, etc., are your personal choice.

Source of heat (see pages 21–23)
Aluminum foil (heavy-duty and regular types)
Can opener
1-quart saucepan with cover

7-inch "no-stick" skillet or frying pan with cover
Spatula
Cooker plate
Coated plastic plates (8-inch size)
Flatware, or disposable plastic type
Sharp knife
Small serving tray
Potholder

Except for the heating device, the approximate cost for these items is six dollars. You need not buy all of them at once; select your recipes and proceed accordingly.

Divide the list when there are two or more girls participating; this cuts the budget tremendously. If you have any of the listed equipment at home, by all means bring it to the office.

Convenience Foods

Any types of food your taste buds crave are available to you, canned or frozen. They're all yours for the selection and preparation.

Canned Foods—Meats, fish, poultry, soups, fruits, vegetables, and desserts are all individually packed in cans of various sizes. For the office, canned foods are your best bet for convenience. Just open, heat, and serve . . . right from the can or onto a plate.

Frozen Foods—Frozen foods should be kept in the freezer unless they are to be thawed. However, you can safely bring certain frozen foods to the office by taking the following precautions:

• Bring only the amount to be used that day; keep remaining portion frozen.
• Freezer fluid cans ("Skotch Ice") help keep foods chilled while traveling. These 6-ounce cans can be used again and again by refreezing. (However, you still need to refrigerate your food on arrival.) Do not open these cans. It's a good idea to mark

this information on the cans when storing them in the freezer; that way they cannot be mistaken for frozen beverages.

- Wrap food securely in foil, place in a paper or insulated bag with a freezer fluid can or other cooling aid. Refrigerate immediately upon arrival at the office. (If you do not have refrigerator facilities available, don't bring frozen foods or other perishable food items at all.)
- Ice cream, sherbet, or any other quick-melting foods should not be transported.
- No cold carrying agent can compete with the temperature of a refrigerator or freezer. Uncooked meats and frozen foods should not be exposed to room temperature for long periods of time. Once food is thawed, *do not refreeze.*

Frozen dinners provide a whole nourishing meal and can be real money-savers for you. There are many appetizing combinations from which to choose—and the price is so right! Although these dinners are well protected with foil wrapping, extra precautions should be taken to avoid leakage as the thawing process begins. Place frozen dinner in a paper bag; close bag, and tie a string across the length and width. Carry it in an upright position and refrigerate immediately upon arrival.

Frozen dinners containing foods that require crisp cooking results should not be used; for example, French-fried potatoes, scallops, and fish sticks. These dinners require an enclosed heat source, such as an oven, in order to get the best results.

To cook frozen dinners in the office, use either of these two easy methods:

1. Heat dinner on a cooker plate over a medium flame for the length of time specified on the package.
2. Fill a large electric skillet with water to ½ inch from rim. Place dinner in water and cook approximately 25 minutes.

Freeze-Dried Foods—You've probably tasted freeze-dried coffee, freeze-dried fruits in packaged breakfast cereals, freeze-dried meats and vegetables in soups made from mixes. This was only a sampling of what is now becoming available to you—it's a whole new world of prepared food. More and more food manufacturers are making use of freeze-dried foods and are starting to distribute their products in the food markets. These foods are lightweight, easy to pack, and can be stored for long periods of time without refrigeration.

Because freeze-dried products are not exposed to the high temperatures of conventional drying methods, they generally retain a truer flavor, color, and nutritive value; their cellular structure is retained, so the product changes little in physical character. The food rehydrates readily because spaces remain where the water was removed.

In addition to individual food items you can now get complete freeze-dried meals. The dinners include a main course, two vegetables, sauce or gravy, and beverage—and yield four generous servings of each course. Simply divide the cost of the meal by four and you have your lunch check for the day—the figure will be incredibly low! Your savings will really soar when you turn to this type of packaged dinner.

For a list of complete freeze-dried meals see Appendix, pages 149–151.

Many camping supply stores stock these foods. Some have mail-order facilities on a national basis. Leon R. Greenman, Inc., at 132 Spring Street, New York, New York 10012, has one of the largest assortments of freeze-dried foods; order forms will be mailed on request.

Fresh Foods—Raw fresh vegetables, fruits, and salad greens can be carried in a plastic bag for easy handling. Bring only foods that can be eaten without cooking.

Leftovers—Make food leftovers from home work for you. This can be a very important part of your overall plan to save dollars. Put the leftover portion in a plastic bag and at lunchtime you can create a new dish by adding other foods or seasonings. But to get leftovers, you have to start somewhere. So we've taken you into your kitchen at home and supplied you with hearty and delicious recipes for meals to enjoy at dinnertime. Then we've followed through with recipes using the leftovers in a different and tasty way for the next day's office lunch.

Portions to Buy

This, of course, depends on how many people are involved in the Office Cook-in Plan. Soups and gravies come in the 10½-ounce can, which is a larger portion than you'd use for yourself for one meal. However, with the group plan it'll disappear fast enough. The 3½- to 5-ounce can is the popular size for one. Canned meats, fish, and spreads are packed in this convenient size. When you find a brand or type of food that appeals to you, buy multiple units at discount prices.

The following guide will help you select the correct size can or jar. Allow ½ cup per serving.

Can or jar size	Serving
3½ to 5 oz.	½ cup
8½ oz.	1 cup
10½ oz.	1¼ cups
12 oz.	1½ cups
1 lb.	2 cups
1 lb. 4 oz.	2½ cups
1 lb. 13 oz.	3½ cups
3 lbs. 2 oz.	6¼ cups

Leftover canned foods can be safely stored in their cans, covered with foil, and refrigerated.

Before you shop, make a list of some of your favorite foods.

When shopping for one, buy the smallest size can or jar.

INITIAL STOCK
 Instant coffee and/or tea
 Powdered milk
 Canned gravy
 Packaged soup mix

Canned condensed soup
Salt
Pepper
Sugar cubes
Catsup
Mustard
Quick-cooking rice
Onion flakes
Lemon juice
Soy sauce
Polyunsaturated vegetable oil or margarine

Except for the margarine, these items can be stored in your desk drawer. Don't overstock! If you don't often use catsup or mustard, for example, don't buy them. At home you can wrap the portion needed for your meal in a little foil and bring it to the office.

As you wander through the supermarket your eyes will feast on all the goodies on the shelves—but stick to the recipes in this book. They are geared to save you fifty percent or more of what your lunch is now costing you.

The "In" Food Group for Well-Balanced Meals

This guide will help you plan your menus as well as keep you in tip-top shape.

FOOD	AVERAGE DAILY SERVING
Milk	1 pint
Meat, fish, and poultry	1 or more servings (liver once a week)
Eggs	1 egg (dried peas or beans may be substituted 3 times a week.)
Vegetables	1 leafy green or yellow and 1 other (serve one raw); 1 potato

Fruits	½ cup citrus fruit or 1 cup tomato juice, plus other fruits (raw, cooked, or canned)
Breads and cereals	3 servings (whole-grain or enriched)
Butter or vitamin-fortified margarine	2 tablespoons

Sources of Cooking Heat

GAS (SELF-CONTAINED)

There are numerous portable self-contained gas-heat devices on the market. Although they have been designed for outdoor cooking, a number of the small portable gas stoves are also excellent for indoor use. They are lightweight, easy to operate, and inexpensive.

The principle by which they operate is exactly the same as that of a butane cigarette lighter. They provide a clean and almost completely odorless flame that gets the job done. You have a stove range on which to place your pan or dish and beneath that is a butane cartridge, which is the fuel source. There is a knob that enables you to adjust the flame just as you would on your range at home. The range or grill is collapsible, therefore making a compact, easy-to-set-up stove that can be readily stored in a filing cabinet or desk drawer.

Most fuel cartridges provide 4 to 6 cooking hours. Using our quick-to-prepare recipes daily, you should get a two- to two-and-a-half-week supply of fuel. Prices for refills range from seventy-five cents to one dollar.

ELECTRICAL COOKING

Before you consider this type of heating device, first check to see if there is an electrical outlet near your desk or wherever you plan to set up. Be sure to read manufacturers' instructions carefully before using any electrical appliance.

Hot Plate—Most of these units have a thermostat regulator for degree of heating. Some have an "off/on" switch; those that do not have to be disconnected after use, or else the unit remains on. The base gets very hot, so do not touch it bare-handed.

The hot plate can be a single- or double-burner unit. The price varies from three to four dollars for the single unit and about eight dollars for the double unit. It can be purchased at most drug and variety stores.

Electric Skillet—The electric skillet can do almost anything from baking to roasting and frying to pan-broiling; it also keeps foods warm for hours. A thermostatic control with an indicator light maintains the proper temperature for perfect cooking and frying results without constant watching. The skillet is large enough to accommodate up to 8 servings. When considering the purchase of this appliance, buy one that has a no-stick finish for easy cleanup and fat-free cooking. Be sure that you have enough space for it, as some of these units are rather bulky in size. A high dome cover is an additional asset for odorless cooking. This is a great item for the group cooking.

Temperature Guide for Electric Skillet

Low	200°F to 300°F
Moderate	300°F to 375°F
Hot	375°F to 400°F

COOKER PLATE

This little metal item is a must in your Office Cook-in Plan. You can heat or cook two or three items at one time without the mess of cleaning a pot. For worry-free cooking, place the cooker plate on a burner. Place your saucepan on it or heat food directly in the can with no worries about sticking or burning. When used over low heat, it keeps food warm without burning it.

Stove-top Baking—For custard cups, apples, potatoes, macaroni, etc., place the baking dish on the cooker plate; invert a small saucepan over the dish; turn the heat on low and bake until done.

Frying—The cooker plate prevents smoke and reduces spatter. It's easy to keep clean—therefore no joints or crevices to collect dirt. To remove stains use any good metal polish. To lift hot, just insert a fork in the vent opening. To prevent warping, avoid extreme heat unless a dish or saucepan is being used on top of it.

Cooking and Storing with Aluminum Foil

Aluminum foil is a handy item for cooking and storing foods. When storing food in the refrigerator or freezer, you can use the lightweight foil. However, if you're planning to bring this food to the office to be heated or cooked, the heavy-duty foil is the better choice.

Foil is the ideal disposable utensil for cooking or heating casseroles, meats, fish, or vegetables. Shape it, cup it, or line a pan with it; cook in it, eat from it, and then throw it away—no fuss, no mess. Foil does not burn; however, fat drippings can ignite on it. Don't use too much foil; use just enough to cover the food or, when cooking in a pan, just line the contour of the pan. Tight sealing is not absolutely necessary as foil retains flavor and moisture. Also, it doesn't matter whether the shiny side of the foil is inside or outside.

ECONOMY TIP

There are many shaped aluminum foil containers, plates, and cooking trays on the market that are reusable and easily cleaned and stored. Save the trays in which frozen dinners or other foods are packaged and use them for your cook-in. Most of these containers are divided into sections, enabling you to cook several different foods at the same time.

Foil for Storage—If you have a refrigerator or water-cooler freezer compartment in the office, you can store cooked leftovers in foil—but plan to use them the next day.

Important Tips for Success

- Plan menus ahead. Try using a variety of foods to make your luncheons interesting and different.

- Don't get too elaborate—remember, you have limited facilities.

- If several people join the Office Cook-in, plan to serve each one the same menu. It's easy to increase ingredients, but preparing different meals gets too involved.

- Experiment on new ideas at home first. Don't invite "kibitzers" or "tasters." It creates too much fuss and upsets the office routine—as well as your boss.

- It's easier to prepare a recipe for two even though you may only need one serving. You can always use the leftover portion the next day. Be creative . . . use it as a side dish or in a sandwich, or add another ingredient to give it a different taste. In this way extra savings are yours because the full portion is used.

- Locate a store near your office where you can buy your supplies instead of carrying them from home daily.

- Remember that you can use frozen items (as directed in this book) only once. Do not save them for the next day unless they have been cooked, and then keep them refrigerated.

- Use a fairly large, heat-resistant tray for standing utensils, hot plates, or hot foods to avoid damage to office furniture.

- Plan to get out of the office after cooking and eating in; you'll need this change of scenery. Since most of the recipes in this book can be prepared in less than fifteen minutes, including setting up, you'll find more time to do other things during your lunch hour.

Measurements

3 teaspoons = 1 tablespoon
4 tablespoons = ¼ cup
8 tablespoons = ½ cup
16 tablespoons = 1 cup
2 cups = 1 pint
2 pints (4 cups) = 1 quart

How to Measure Liquids—Place measuring cup on a table. Pour in liquid up to proper mark. Bend down and look at mark at eye level to make sure it is right.

Spoon Measurement—To measure small amounts, pack food on a measuring spoon. Level off with a straight-edged spatula or the back of a table knife.

Can Measurements—

1 can	(vegetables and fruits)	7½ to 8½ ounces
1 can	(soups)	10½ ounces
1 can	(fish, meats, spreads)	3½ to 5 ounces
1 large can	(sauces, macaroni, spaghetti, etc.)	15 ounces

Pertinent Cooking Terms

Bake   To cook in a heated oven. ("Roast" is the same process, but applies to meat.)

Baste   To moisten food while cooking by spooning on liquid or fat.

Beat   To make a mixture smooth, usually with a hand or electric beater.

Blend   To combine two or more ingredients well, usually with a spoon.

Boil   To cook in hot, bubbling liquid (212°F). Slow boiling refers to gentle bubbling, rapid boiling to vigorous bubbling.

Braise   To brown meat slowly and well on all sides in hot fat, then adding liquid to cover and simmering covered, over low heat.

Broil   To cook under direct heat, in a broiler or over hot coals, or between two heated surfaces.

Chill   To place in a refrigerator or other cold place until cold.

Chop   To cut food into small pieces with a knife or chopper.

Coat   To cover an entire surface with a given mixture.

Cube   To cut into small cubes, usually about ½ inch in size.

Dice   To cut into very small cubes, usually about ¼ inch in size.

Dissolve   To mix a dry substance with a liquid until it is in solution.

Dot   To scatter small bits, usually of shortening or a dry ingredient, of food.

Fry   To cook in hot fat.

Grease   To rub lightly with butter, margarine, shortening, or salad oil.

Panbroil   To cook uncovered in an ungreased or lightly greased hot skillet, pouring off fat as it cooks out.

Pare   To remove an outer covering, usually of fruits and vegetables.

Peel   To strip off an outer covering, usually of fruits.

Shred   To tear or cut into thin pieces or strips.

Simmer   To cook in liquid just below boiling point, using low heat to maintain temperature.

Stir   To blend ingredients with a slow, circular motion, widening the circles until all ingredients are well blended.

Tenderize   To cook until a fork pierces food easily.

Toast   To brown lightly, in a broiler, oven, or toaster, or over hot coals.

2

Situation Menus and Recipes

The Office Dynamo Menu

When I'm really busy on the job, a meal like this helps me avoid that midday feeling of fatigue that the rest of the girls go through.

> Soup
> Roast Beef and Rice
> Sliced tomatoes
> Potato chips
> Chocolate layer cake
> Beverage

WHAT YOU NEED
2 slices cooked roast beef   *1 teaspoon soy sauce*
⅓ cup water   *1 tablespoon catsup*
⅓ cup quick-cooking rice   *½ teaspoon onion flakes*

HOW TO DO IT
Cut roast beef slices into strips. In a saucepan boil water; stir in

rice. Cover and remove from heat; let stand 5 minutes. Stir in soy sauce, catsup, onion flakes, and beef strips. Heat over a low flame 2 minutes. *Serves 1.*

The "She's a Lousy Typist but Boy, Can She Cook" Menu

Until I become a more experienced typist, I think I'll plan menus like this and make an extra portion for tasters who pass by—like the boss.

Salmon and Zucchini Omelet
Onion sticks
Peachy shortcake
Beverage

WHAT YOU NEED

2 eggs
1 3½-ounce can pink salmon
1 tablespoon salad oil
1 8½-ounce can zucchini
1 teaspoon lemon juice

HOW TO DO IT

Break eggs into a bowl and beat with a fork. Flake salmon, removing bones and skin; combine with eggs. In a skillet heat oil; add egg mixture and heat through slowly, lifting mixture as it sets. Slowly add zucchini and half of the liquid from the can (discard remaining portion). Stir lightly, letting liquid flow under egg-and-salmon mixture. Add lemon juice. Heat over a low flame 2 minutes more. *Serves 2.*

The Hangover Menu

Thank heaven I can do this in the quiet and privacy of my own office. Oh, my head!

> Tomato juice
> Egg, any style
> Toast
> Black coffee
> 2 aspirins

WHAT YOU NEED
1 *egg*   2 *slices bread*

HOW TO DO IT
Cook egg to your preference. Toast bread. Relax and you'll feel better in no time. *Serves 1.*

The "I'm Going Off My Diet" Menu

Today is a special day and I want to eat something special. I've lost a few pounds and saved a few dollars with my Office Cook-in Plan . . . so I'm entitled.

> Chicken à la King with Mexican Corn
> Toast
> Raisin pound cake
> Beverage

WHAT YOU NEED
2 *slices white bread*   1 *8½-ounce can Mexican corn,*
1 *4½-ounce can Chicken à la King*   *drained*

HOW TO DO IT
Toast bread; place toast on serving plates. In a saucepan combine

chicken and corn. Stir and heat over a low flame about 8 minutes. Serve hot over toast. *Serves 1.*

The "I'm Going Back on My Diet" Menu

The Office Cook-in is the best way to lose weight. I can eat only what I bring!

> Bouillon
> Tuna and Tomato Salad
> Melba toast
> Raisin and custard pudding
> Beverage

WHAT YOU NEED

1 3¼-ounce can water-packed tuna
1 tomato, sliced
½ cup cottage cheese

½ cucumber, peeled and thinly sliced

HOW TO DO IT

Drain and flake tuna; place equal portions on each tomato slice. Top with cottage cheese balls and surround with cucumber slices. *Serves 1.*

The Lazy-Day Menu

Just a few minutes till lunchtime—but who wants to cook? I've been slaving over a hot typewriter all morning!

> Tomato juice
> Frank 'n' Beans
> Fruit-raisin cup
> Beverage

1 frankfurter, precooked variety   *1 roll*
½ 8½-ounce can sauerkraut   *½ 8½-ounce can pork 'n' beans*

How to Do It
Place frank in roll and top with sauerkraut; wrap in foil. Place frank and opened can of pork 'n' beans on a cooker plate and heat over a medium flame 5 to 8 minutes. *Serves 1.*

The "Girls Down the Hall Are Stopping By" Menu

It's got to be something I know they'll enjoy—and besides, it's one of my favorite dishes too!

> Meatballs and Spaghetti
> Italian bread
> Custard pudding

What You Need
1 32-ounce can meatballs in sauce   *3 cups cooked spaghetti*
1 16-ounce can tomato sauce   *¼ cup Parmesan cheese*

How to Do It
In a skillet combine meatballs and tomato sauce. Add cooked spaghetti. Stir and heat over a medium flame 10 minutes. Top with Parmesan cheese and serve hot. *Serves 4.*

The High-Tension Menu

When things don't go the way you want them to and tension starts to mount, even the best meal loses its appeal. You need a quick and easy-to-digest lunch—and here it is.

Vegetable Plate
Crackers
Vanilla pudding
Beverage

WHAT YOU NEED
1 8½-ounce can sliced carrots   1 8½-ounce can whole-kernel corn
1 8½-ounce can green lima beans   Salt and pepper to taste

HOW TO DO IT
Open all cans and drain liquids. Place carrots, beans, and corn in foil. Close foil and heat through about 5 minutes. Add salt and pepper to taste. Serve hot. *Serves 1.*

The "I'm Out to Trap the Office Bachelor" Menu

With a menu like this I know I'll pass the taste test—that puts me on first base with him!

Onion soup
Chicken and Spanish Rice
Rye bread
Apple rings with cinnamon
Beverage

WHAT YOU NEED

1 5-ounce can boned chicken
1 8½-ounce can Spanish rice

2 tablespoons Parmesan cheese
4 or 5 pitted black olives

HOW TO DO IT

Drain and flake chicken. In a saucepan heat Spanish rice over a medium flame. Add chicken and 1 tablespoon Parmesan cheese; heat 3 minutes more. Pour onto a serving plate; sprinkle with remaining cheese and surround with olives. *Serves 1.*

1592705

The Rainy-Day Menu

Rainy days are a drag—everyone orders "the usual," which is late in arriving and gets colder every minute. But your freshly cooked, appetizing meal is the envy of everyone on a day like this!

Soup
Chili con Carne with Franks and Spinach
Jelly doughnut
Beverage

WHAT YOU NEED

1 8½-ounce can chili con carne
1 8-ounce can frankfurters, drained

1 8½-ounce can chopped spinach, drained

HOW TO DO IT

In a saucepan heat chili con carne and franks over a medium flame about 8 minutes, stirring occasionally. Add spinach and heat 3 minutes more. Serve hot. (Spinach can also be made as a side dish by placing it in foil and cooking it along with the rest.) *Serves 1.*

The "I Can't Adjust the Air Conditioner and I'm Freezing" Menu

There's nothing like a hot cooked meal to stop my teeth from chattering to the tune of my typing keys.

> Soup
> Hot Turkey Sandwich with Gravy and Hot Pineapple Slices
> Hot chocolate

WHAT YOU NEED

1 3-ounce package sliced smoked turkey
2 slices bread

½ 8¼-ounce can sliced pineapple, drained
½ 16-ounce can giblet gravy

HOW TO DO IT

Arrange turkey slices on bread; top with pineapple slices. In a saucepan heat gravy over a medium flame about 3 minutes or until hot, stirring constantly. Pour over sandwich and serve. *Serves 1.*

The Working Late Menu

Thank heaven I was prepared for this! This dinner menu is worth double the price at this time of night.

> Creamed Vienna Sausages with Peas and Onions
> Salad greens
> Roll
> Fruit tart
> Beverage

WHAT YOU NEED

½ 10½-ounce can cream of mushroom soup
¼ cup milk
1 4-ounce can Vienna sausages,
   drained

1 8½-ounce can peas and onions,
   drained
Salt and pepper to taste

HOW TO DO IT

In a saucepan blend soup and milk; add remaining ingredients. Heat, stirring constantly. *Serves 1.*

NOTE: Save leftovers in refrigerator and create a new dish for the next day's lunch.

The Office Gourmet Menu

I'd like to correct the mistaken impression that most people have about gourmet cooks. They are not to be found only in expensive restaurants or townhouses—a gourmet cook may be just a typewriter away from you!

Cranberry juice cocktail
Curried Chicken with Peanuts
Soft roll
Bed of grapes
Beverage

WHAT YOU NEED

1 5-ounce can boned chicken
1 tablespoon crushed salted peanuts
¼ teaspoon curry powder

½ 10½-ounce can cheddar cheese
   soup
1 8½-ounce can peas, drained

HOW TO DO IT

Drain and flake chicken. In a saucepan combine all ingredients. Heat over a low flame about 8 minutes, stirring often. *Serves 1.*

The "Executive Lunch for Nonexecutives" Menu

Imagine an expense-account meal within my working-girl budget!

> Tossed green and vegetable salad
> Minute Steak
> Potato chips
> Roll
> Hot applesauce with marshmallows
> Beverage

WHAT YOU NEED

1 *tablespoon margarine*   1 *tablespoon prepared mustard*
½ *pound minute steak*

HOW TO DO IT

In a skillet melt margarine and brown one side of steak. Spread half of the mustard on the uncooked side. Cook 2 minutes more, then turn and cook on the other side about 5 minutes. Spread with remaining mustard and serve. *Serves 1.*

The "I Can't Cook but They'll Never Know It" Menu

Everyone tells me I'm a great cook! I'm certainly not going to tell them that the recipes in this book are a snap to prepare.

> Beef Chow Mein
> Chunk pineapple cup
> Fortune cookies
> Beverage

WHAT YOU NEED

⅓ cup water

⅓ cup quick-cooking rice

1 16-ounce can beef chow mein

1 3-ounce box chow mein noodles

2 tablespoons soy sauce

Salt to taste

HOW TO DO IT

In a saucepan bring water to a boil; stir in rice. Cover and remove from heat; let stand 5 minutes. In foil place chow mein, noodles, and soy sauce. Close foil tightly and heat on a cooker plate over a medium flame about 10 minutes. Serve over rice. Add salt to taste and more soy sauce, if desired. *Serves 2.*

The "Air Conditioner Is Broken" Menu

Cooking and eating in can be uncomfortable when the air conditioner goes on the blink. But if you're flexible enough, lunch can be refreshing—and cool.

> Cold vegetable juice
> Shrimp and Tomato Salad
> Crackers
> Iced tea

What You Need

Leaves from 1/4 head lettuce
1 4½-ounce can medium shrimp

2 tablespoons mayonnaise
1 tomato, cut into wedges

How to Do It

Tear some of the lettuce leaves into small pieces. Combine with shrimp and mayonnaise; add tomato wedges. Serve on remaining lettuce leaves. *Serves 1.*

3

Soups and Sandwiches

A serving of hot soup and a sandwich makes a nutritious meal any time. The variety of sandwich combinations is endless, and all you have to do is select your favorite filling. If you are a sandwich-for-lunch lover (and who isn't?), you can really profit, with savings of fifty percent or more, by doing it yourself. In our survey we have estimated the cost of homemade sandwiches against that of the same sandwiches from the local coffee shop or restaurant. (This does not include beverage and dessert, which can easily be half of the total cost of the sandwich.)

Type of Sandwich	Restaurant Price	Prepared at Home
Chopped egg	$ .90	$ .25
Tuna fish	.95	.35
Salmon	1.15	.50
Boiled ham	1.25	.60
Bacon-lettuce-tomato	1.10	.50
Grilled ham and cheese	1.25	.60
Hot turkey	1.50	.65
Hot roast beef	1.75	.80
Hamburger	.95	.25
Western	1.10	.35

Comparing the prices, you'll note the considerable savings. Here's how you can start your savings plan with a Soup-and-Sandwich Week.

Plan your Soup-and-Sandwich menus for the week and shop for the foods needed. One loaf of enriched or whole-wheat bread will yield more than the ten slices you'll need to prepare the sandwiches. Select your favorite spreads, canned meats and fish, cheeses, eggs, and other favorite fillings; remember to buy only the amount you will use. For extra savings use leftover chicken, beef, fish, and luncheon meats.

PACKING TIPS
- When using spreads don't let the fillings ooze over the edges of the bread. Wrap sandwiches individually in foil or wax paper and secure tightly. Sandwiches can be stored in the freezer; by the time you get to work, the sandwich will be thawed out and ready to eat at lunchtime. For a big time-saver, make your sandwiches ahead for the week.
- Avoid lettuce and tomatoes in sandwiches prepared in advance; they become limp and unappetizing. Wash them, place in a plastic bag, and refrigerate; add them to the sandwich when you're ready to eat.
- If you are ambitious enough to carry a thermos back and forth to work, heat your soup or beverage in the morning before leaving and fill the thermos. However, it's just as easy to do it in the office. Many offices have a hot-water attachment to the water cooler, making the job very easy . . . just add dehydrated soup flakes to a cup of hot water, stir, and enjoy.

A NOTE ABOUT TOASTING BREAD
Toasted bread can vary the taste of your sandwiches. Office toasting can be done this way:
- The quickest and most efficient way we found is by using an old camping method. Insert a fork firmly in the center of the bread. Toast bread one inch over a medium flame, being careful not to burn it. Toast the other side and you have hot toast in less than thirty seconds.

- A sandwich wire broiler with a handle is an ideal tool. Just insert the bread, close the mesh top, and hold the broiler one inch above a medium flame. Turn bread over and toast the other side.
- The old-fashioned toaster is back and sells for about $1. It can toast one to four slices at a time. Just place the bread on each side of toaster; when one side is done, turn the bread over. It can be placed directly on flame.
- If it's hard for you to plan ahead, don't let that stop you from your office lunch-in. Wrap two pieces of bread in foil, add a can of tuna or spread, throw in a piece of fresh fruit and a small can of juice, and you're all set. If all these items happen to be on your pantry shelf, that lunch will cost zero.

Sandwich Meats

Cold cuts and luncheon meats provide a large variety of sandwiches. Serve one with your favorite hot soup for a really satisfying meal. Any of these meats can be cut up, diced, or combined with one another.

Roast beef, turkey, pastrami, corned beef, and chicken can be bought precooked. Don't let the price of dollars per pound scare you; you can buy as little as two ounces, which is enough for a sandwich, for approximately fifty to sixty-five cents. This cost is still half of the restaurant price for the same type of sandwich.

Smoked turkey, corned beef, ham, chicken, and pastrami are delicious and economical purchases for sandwiches. A three-ounce package yields enough for two sandwiches at a cost of less than forty-five cents. These meats are sliced extra thin and can be used in egg, rice, or noodle dishes, or in dips or salads.

HOT SANDWICHES

Hero Sandwich

½ 16-ounce can meatballs   ¼ loaf French bread
3 tablespoons pizza-flavored catsup

Drain liquid from meatballs. In a saucepan mash meatballs and
add catsup. Stir and heat over a medium flame about 5 minutes.
Cut bread open and hollow out the center. Spread mixture onto
bread. *Serves 1.*

Grilled Ham and Cheese

2 slices boiled ham   2 slices bread
1 slice American cheese

Place ham and cheese on 2 pieces of bread. Wrap securely in foil.
Place on a cooker plate and heat each side about 5 minutes.
Serves 1.

Frankfurter and Bun

1 frankfurter, precooked   1 bun

Wrap frankfurter in foil and place directly on a cooker plate
over a medium flame about 5 minutes. Open bun and lay flat on
cooker plate; heat until toasted. *Serves 1.*

Sloppy Joe

2 hamburger buns   1 16-ounce can Sloppy Joe meat
                                    mixture

Place buns in foil; pour on Sloppy Joe mixture. Heat on a
cooker plate for 10 minutes, or until hot. *Serves 2.*

Hot Meat Loaf Sandwich

1 slice meat loaf   4 tablespoons catsup
1 slice bread

Place meat loaf slice on a piece of bread; top with 4 tablespoons
catsup. Wrap in foil and heat on a cooker plate about 10 minutes. *Serves 1.*

Open-Face Sandwich

1 8½-ounce can pork and beans   2 slices bread
4 slices bologna

Open can of pork and beans and place can on a cooker plate; heat
10 minutes. Place 2 slices bologna on each slice of bread. When
beans are hot, pour over sandwiches. *Serves 2.*

Gravy Magic

Quick-heating hot gravy poured over a meat sandwich can make a whole meal. Add a vegetable or a salad and you've got the equivalent of an expensive restaurant lunch with enormous savings.

Gravy comes either in the canned condensed form or as a packaged mix. If you are cooking for one, use the mix, which may yield more than you need but is more convenient to store.

GRAVY MIX

Combine half the contents of a 7/8-ounce package gravy mix with 1/2 cup water in a small saucepan. Cook over medium heat, stirring constantly, until gravy comes to a boil; simmer 1 minute. Yields 1/2 cup.

CANNED GRAVY

Canned gravy is your best bet when cooking for two or three. Just pour it in a saucepan and heat until hot.

Both kinds of gravy come in a variety of flavors and are delicious over rice, noodles, or mashed potatoes as well as sandwiches.

HAMBURGERS

Hamburger (ground beef) is one of the most popular selections on a luncheon menu. This meat is highly perishable, so buy it fresh and store it well.

POINTS TO REMEMBER
- Handle ground beef as little as possible. The less handling it gets, the juicier and more tender it will be.

- To make patties pat meat loosely into shape. Do not flatten patties with a spatula.
- To store patties wrap them loosely in wax paper, leaving the ends open, and refrigerate immediately. Use within two days.
- To store patties in freezer wrap them individually in foil and close tightly. This way they will keep two to three months.
- One pound of ground beef will yield five good-sized patties.

Office Hamburger

Before leaving for the office, place foil-wrapped frozen patty in a bag with a freezer fluid can; refrigerate upon arrival. At lunchtime the patty will be thawed and ready to cook. Canned hamburgers and frozen patties are available at most stores. These are very convenient to use and quite tasty. Place foil-wrapped patty on a cooker plate or in a pan and cook over medium flame 5 minutes. Open foil; turn patty over and cook 5 minutes more, or to desired doneness. Place on a hamburger bun. To heat bun, place a piece of foil under it and place on top of patty while second side is cooking.

Cheeseburger

1 *hamburger bun*
1 *teaspoon prepared mustard*

1 *hamburger patty*
1 *slice American cheese*

Cut bun open and spread mustard on. Place hamburger patty on one bun half. Wrap tightly in foil and cook over a medium flame 5 minutes. Open foil and turn patty over. Place cheese slice on patty and cover with other bun half. Cook 5 minutes more. *Serves 1.*

Tasty Burger

1 *hamburger bun*
1 *tablespoon mayonnaise*

1 *tablespoon pickled relish*
1 *hamburger patty*

Cut bun open; spread mayonnaise on one half, pickled relish on the other. Cook foil-wrapped patty over a medium flame 5 minutes. Open foil, turn patty over. Place bun half spread with relish on top and cook 5 minutes more. When done, close sandwich with other bun half. *Serves 1.*

Mexican Burger

1 *16-ounce can meatballs*
½ *8½-ounce can chopped green chili or chili con carne*

2 *hamburger buns*

Drain liquid from meatballs. In a saucepan heat meatballs and chili over a medium flame about 5 minutes. Spoon onto hamburger buns. *Serves 2.*

French Hamburger

½ *16-ounce can meatballs*
1 *teaspoon onion flakes*

¼ *loaf French bread*
2 *tablespoons French dressing*

Open canned meatballs; place can on a cooker plate and heat 5 minutes. Stir in onion flakes. Cut bread open and hollow out center; spread on dressing. Drain liquid from cooked meatballs and spoon meatballs onto bread. *Serves 1.*

Bar-B-Q Hamburger

1 *hamburger patty*   1 *hamburger bun*
1/4 *cup barbeque sauce*

Open foil-wrapped patty and add sauce. Close foil tightly and cook patty over a medium flame 7 minutes. Open foil and turn patty over; cook 5 minutes more. Set aside and toast bun. Place patty and sauce on bun. *Serves 1.*

QUICK SOUPS

Soup Mixes

Instant soup and broth mixes are delicious and convenient to use. Just dissolve the contents of one packet in six ounces of hot water and you have a good midmorning or late-afternoon booster. When preparing dehydrated soup mixes, two full tablespoons of mix yield one cup of soup. For extra flavor, add meat, vegetables, croutons, or crackers.

Canned Soups

Since most canned condensed soups come in the 10 1/2-ounce size, one can will yield portions for three or four. All you have to do in most cases is add one canful of water to contents of can. In addition, any of the creamed soups can be made into sauces just by adding milk.

With canned soups, any unused portion can be preserved by covering the can tightly with foil and refrigerating. However, it should be used the next day.

Minestrone-Plus Soup

1 10½-ounce can minestrone soup   1 soup can water
1 8½-ounce can macaroni and
   cheese

In a saucepan combine all ingredients; heat, stirring occasionally.
Serve hot with crackers. *Serves 2.*

Chinese Turkey Soup

1 10½-ounce can turkey-vegetable   1 teaspoon soy sauce
   soup   ½ cup chow chow mein noodles
½ soup can water

In a saucepan combine soup, water, and soy sauce. Heat until hot.
Top with noodles and serve. *Serves 2.*

Onion Soup

2 cups water   2 tablespoons Parmesan cheese
½ 1⅜-ounce package onion soup
   mix

In a saucepan boil water; stir in soup mix. Cover and simmer 10
minutes, stirring occasionally. Top with Parmesan cheese and
serve hot. (You can add croutons, French bread cubes, or cooked
rice for extra flavor.) *Serves 2.*

Pea Soup with Franks

2 cups water
1 2-ounce package green pea soup
  mix

2 frankfurters, cooked and thinly
  sliced

In a saucepan boil water. Add soup mix, stirring occasionally until smooth. Add franks; cover and simmer 4 to 5 minutes. *Serves 2.*

Vegetable and Meatball Soup

1 10½-ounce can vegetable soup
½ soup can water

8 leftover cooked meatballs or 1
  pound canned meatballs

In a saucepan stir in soup and water. Heat to full boil, stirring occasionally. Add meatballs and simmer 3 to 4 minutes. *Serves 2.*

Cheddar Cheese and Mushroom Soup

1 10½-ounce can condensed cheddar cheese soup
1 soup can water

1 3-ounce can sliced mushrooms,
  drained
½ cup croutons or 1 slice toasted
  bread, cubed

In a saucepan stir in soup. Add water gradually, stirring constantly. Heat to boiling, stirring occasionally; remove from heat. Add mushrooms and croutons or bread cubes and serve hot. *Serves 2.*

Chicken Noodle and Vienna Sausage Soup

1 10½-ounce can chicken noodle
   soup
¾ soup can water

1 4-ounce can Vienna sausage
1 teaspoon parsley flakes
½ teaspoon soy sauce (optional)

In a saucepan combine soup and water. Heat to boiling, stirring occasionally. Add remaining ingredients and heat over a low flame 3 minutes more. *Serves 2.*

Clam Chowder Special

1 10½-ounce can New England
   clam chowder
1 soup can milk

1 8½-ounce can mixed vegetables,
   drained

In a saucepan empty in soup and gradually add milk; stir. Heat slowly, stirring constantly, but do not boil. Add vegetables and heat 1 minute longer. *Serves 2.*

Tomato and Tuna Soup

1 10½-ounce can tomato soup
¾ soup can water

1 3¼-ounce can chunk tuna,
   drained

In a saucepan stir in soup and water; heat to boiling, stirring occasionally. Add tuna and heat 1 minute over a low flame. Serve with crackers, melba toast, zwieback, or onion sticks. *Serves 2.*

4

Eggs and Cheese

THE EGG AND YOU

It's hard to believe one little egg can contribute so much to our daily health requirements. Eggs are an excellent source of protein minerals, iron, calcium, phosphorous, niacin, and vitamins A, B_1, B_2, and D.

Eggs are perishable items and should be refrigerated as soon as possible. Carrying eggs to the office can be tricky, so do it carefully. Split an empty egg carton in half; wrap eggs in foil and place in carton. This should insure the protection needed en route. If eggs are dropped and do break, the foil will act as a container. Place eggs in refrigerator as soon as you get to the office.

SHORTCUT HINT: Hard-cooked eggs can be precooked at home.

Hard-Cooked Eggs

In a saucepan place egg whole in 2½ inches water. Cover pan and bring water to boil over high heat. Reduce heat and cook 7 minutes more. Remove pan from heat and let stand about 5 minutes. Run cold water in pan; remove eggshell by cracking the surface gently.

Poached Eggs

Fill the bottom pan of an egg poacher with water halfway. Break egg gently into poacher. Cover and heat 5 minutes. Use a knife to remove edges and turn egg onto a serving dish.

Scrambled Eggs

In a bowl beat 2 or more eggs lightly with fork. Pour eggs into a "nonstick"-coated skillet. (If an ordinary skillet is used, melt enough butter to cover bottom.) Cook over a low flame until light and moist, lifting mixture with a spoon as it sets.

Fried Eggs

Break eggs into a cup, one at a time, being careful not to break yolks; pour gently into a "nonstick"-coated skillet (or into an ordinary skillet in which enough butter has been melted to cover bottom). Cover and cook over a low flame 3 minutes. To cook other side, carefully turn eggs and cook 1 minute longer.

Tuna Omelet

2 eggs
1 3¼-ounce can chunk white tuna

1 small green pepper, chopped

In a bowl mix eggs and pepper. Pour mixture into a "nonstick"-coated skillet (or into an ordinary skillet in which enough butter has been melted to cover bottom). Cook slowly over a low flame until partially set; add tuna. Continue cooking, lifting mixture as it sets. Serve hot with toast or rolls. *Serves 1.*

Egg Salad

2 eggs, hard-cooked
2 tablespoons mayonnaise
Salt and pepper to taste

1 teaspoon onion flakes
1 large lettuce leaf

Remove eggshells; in a bowl mash eggs fine. Add mayonnaise, salt and pepper, and onion flakes; mix well. Serve on lettuce leaf or combine into a sandwich. *Serves 1.*

Scrambled Eggs and Sausages

2 eggs
1 4-ounce can cooked and sliced
  pork sausages

2 tablespoons salad oil
2 tablespoons catsup

In a bowl combine eggs and sausages. Heat oil in a skillet; add egg mixture and top with catsup. Heat slowly, lifting mixture as it sets. *Serves 1.*

French Toast

2 *eggs*   *Salt and pepper to taste*
2 *slices bread*

Break eggs onto a plate and beat with a fork in a circular motion. Dip both sides of each bread slice into eggs and place bread in a heated "nonstick"-coated skillet (or in an ordinary skillet in which enough butter has been melted to cover bottom). Sprinkle with salt and pepper. Cook each side until nicely browned. *Serves 1.*

Egg and Corned Beef Patty

1 *egg*   3 *tablespoons catsup*
1 *8-ounce can corned beef hash*

Break egg into a cup and set aside. Mix hash and catsup and shape into a large patty. In a "nonstick"-coated skillet brown patty on both sides. (If an ordinary skillet is used, melt enough butter to cover bottom.) Glide egg onto patty in skillet; cover and heat 5 minutes. *Serves 1.*

Ham and Eggs

2 *eggs*   1 *tablespoon herb-seasoned crou-*
½ *cup deviled diced ham*   *tons*

In a bowl mix eggs and ham. Heat croutons and add to egg mixture. Pour mixture into a "nonstick"-coated skillet (or an ordinary skillet in which enough butter has been melted to cover bottom). Cook slowly over a low flame, lifting mixture as it sets. *Serves 1.*

Eggs Benedict

1 *English muffin, split in half*
2 *slices boiled ham*
2 *eggs*

¾ *cup water*
½ *1⅝-ounce package Hollandaise sauce mix*

Toast muffin halves; place a ham slice on each half. Fill each compartment of a three-in-one skillet with ¼ cup water. Heat water to boiling; break eggs and drop one in each of two compartments. Add Hollandaise sauce mix gradually in third. Cover skillet and cook over a low flame, stirring sauce until thickened. Turn poached eggs onto muffin halves and spoon on sauce. *Serves 2.*

Scrambled Eggs Creole

2 *eggs*
1 *teaspoon onion flakes*
1 *tablespoon salad oil*

1 *8½-ounce can stewed tomatoes, drained*
Salt and pepper to taste

In a bowl mix eggs and onion flakes. Heat oil in a skillet and pour in eggs; cook slowly, lifting mixture as it sets. Add tomatoes and fold eggs over them. Cook 3 minutes more; season to taste and serve hot. *Serves 1.*

Egg Foo Yung

2 eggs
2 tablespoons mayonnaise
1 teaspoon soy sauce

1 tablespoon onion flakes
1 tablespoon salad oil
½ cup mushroom gravy

In a bowl combine eggs and mayonnaise until well blended. Add soy sauce and onion flakes. In a skillet heat oil; pour in egg mixture and cook over a low flame until set. Turn and cook on other side. Pour in gravy and heat 5 minutes longer. *Serves 2.*

Egg and Vegetable Plate

2 eggs, hard-cooked
1 8½-ounce can mixed vegetables, drained

1 8½-ounce can creamed corn

Remove eggshells; slice eggs and place on a plate. In a saucepan combine mixed vegetables and corn; heat slowly and pour over eggs. Serve with toast or English muffins. *Serves 2.*

Egg and Macaroni Plate

1 egg, hard-cooked
1 8¼-ounce can macaroni and cheese

1 teaspoon onion flakes
Dash paprika

Remove eggshell and slice egg. In a saucepan heat macaroni and cheese until hot; add onion flakes. Pour onto a plate, place egg slices around edges, and top with paprika. *Serves 1.*

Mushroom Omelet

2 eggs
1 teaspoon soy sauce
Salt and pepper to taste

1 tablespoon salad oil
1 3-ounce can sliced mushrooms,
drained

Break eggs into a bowl and beat lightly. Add soy sauce and salt and pepper. In a skillet heat oil; add eggs and cook over a low flame, lifting edges as eggs set. Remove to a plate; place mushrooms in center of omelet and fold edges over. Serve hot. *Serves 2.*

(From this basic omelet you can create many variations. Try *stewed tomatoes, your favorite vegetable, luncheon meats, bacon, or cheese.)*

Deviled Egg Salad

1 egg, hard-cooked
1 2¼-ounce can deviled ham
spread

2 slices toast

Remove eggshell. In a cup mash egg and ham spread together with a fork. Spread mixture on toast. *Serves 1.*

Egg Squares

12 slices white bread, crusts
    removed
2 tablespoons margarine
3 hard-cooked eggs, shelled and
    mashed

¼ cup mayonnaise
2 teaspoons horseradish-mustard
Dash salt
Dash curry powder

Spread each bread slice with margarine. Mix eggs, mayonnaise, horseradish-mustard, salt, and curry powder in a small bowl. Spread mixture over 6 of the bread slices; cover with remaining slices to make sandwiches. When ready to serve, cut each sandwich into quarters. *Yields 24 squares.*

NOTE: Sandwiches can be made at home and cut into squares at serving time.

CHEESE

Cottage, cream, Swiss, American, and other processed cheeses all provide quick and nutritious lunches. Eat them plain or in sandwiches, or combine with meat, spreads, salads, fruits, or jellies.

Cheese, with crackers and hot bouillon or soup, makes a great pick-me-up to beat eleven-o'clock hunger or four-o'clock fatigue. Try it instead of the usual dull coffee or tea syndrome.

Most cheese must be kept refrigerated and should be rewrapped tightly and used as soon as possible after opening.

Cheese Roll-ups

1 2¼-ounce can deviled ham
   spread (or any luncheon meat)

4 slices American cheese
2 slices bread

Spread ham in equal amounts on each cheese slice. Toast bread and cut diagonally into strips. Place strips on top of ham. Roll up and secure with toothpicks. *Serves 2.*

Mini Spaghetti with Cheese Sauce

8 quarts water
2 tablespoons salt

1 1-pound box extra-thin spaghetti
1 tablespoon margarine

In each of two large pans bring 4 quarts of water to a boil; add 1 tablespoon salt to water into each pan. Break spaghetti strands from one package into thirds and add slowly to water in first pan. Repeat with second package of spaghetti for other pan. Boil 9 to 12 minutes, depending on desired tenderness, stirring often. Drain thoroughly in a colander. When cooled, place in a bowl; mix in margarine and refrigerate overnight. Make Cheese Sauce in the office. *Serves 4.*

Cheese Sauce

1 10½-ounce cheddar cheese soup
¼ cup milk

Dash salt and pepper
¼ teaspoon paprika

In a saucepan stir in soup until smooth; gradually blend in milk and add remaining ingredients. Heat, stirring often.

Arrange spaghetti in a chafing dish or casserole with a warming ladle. Pour in cheese sauce and mix well. *Serves 10.*

Pizza Bits

3 packages frozen pizza circles (4
  circles each)

1 16-ounce can spaghetti sauce
4 tablespoons Parmesan cheese

Cut each pizza circle into quarters. Place pizza bits in an electric skillet and heat at 350° for 10 minutes. Top each pizza bit with ½ teaspoon spaghetti sauce and dash Parmesan cheese. Heat 5 minutes more. Serve right from the skillet or on a heated tray. *Yields 48 bits.*

Quick Cheese Fondue

1 10½-ounce can frozen cream of
  shrimp soup, thawed

¼ teaspoon curry
1 cup diced sharp American cheese

In a saucepan combine soup, curry powder, and cheese. Cook over a cooker plate or a pan of boiling water until cheese melts, stirring constantly.

Serve with small chunks of French bread or bread sticks, to be dipped in cheese mixture. *Serves 4.*

NOTE: To keep fondue hot, as it should be when served, keep on cooker plate over a low flame.

Swiss Cheese Fondue

2 cloves garlic
3 10½-ounce cans frozen cream of shrimp soup, thawed

3 cups finely shredded Swiss cheese
½ cup dry white wine

Rub a chafing dish or the top pan of a double boiler with garlic cloves; discard garlic. Add soup and cheese. Heat until cheese melts. Stir in wine.

Serve with small chunks of French bread or cocktail franks, to be dipped in cheese mixture. *Serves 10.*

Muffin Cheese Pizza

1 6-ounce can tomato paste
2 English muffins, split in half
2 tablespoons Parmesan cheese

2 slices sharp American cheese, each cut into 4 strips

Spread tomato paste on English muffin halves and top with Parmesan cheese. Crisscross 2 strips American cheese onto each half. Wrap muffins in foil and cook over a medium flame 8 to 10 minutes, or until cheese melts. *Serves 2.*

5

Fish

When buying fish select any of the frozen or canned varieties. Frozen fish must be thawed before cooking; keep it refrigerated during the thawing process and cook the same day. Your best bet for office cooking is the precoated, preseasoned variety (fillets, sticks, cakes, etc.), which can be heated within fifteen minutes; just read manufacturers' instructions on packages. To bring frozen fish to the office, wrap in foil, only the portion to be used that day, and refrigerate immediately on arrival.

You have an equally vast selection of canned fish. Tuna, salmon, crabmeat, herring, and sardines are among the more popular varieties. Serve them directly from the can or in sandwiches or salads, accompanied by soup; or use them to prepare any of the following recipes.

Fried Scallops in Newburg Sauce

3 7-ounce packages frozen fried
scallops

1 10-ounce can Newburg sauce

Preheat oven to 375°. Place scallops on a cookie sheet about 1 inch apart. Heat 15 to 20 minutes.

In a chafing dish heat Newburg sauce until very hot; add scallops. Serve hot, with toothpicks. *Serves 10.*

NOTE: Prepare scallops at home and bring to the office in a tightly covered container; keep refrigerated until ready to use. Make Newburg sauce in the office.

Tuna and Rice with Mushrooms

5 tablespoons margarine
4 7½-ounce cans tuna, drained
2 10½-ounce cans cream of mushroom soup
4½ cups hot water
4 cups quick-cooking rice

1 6-ounce can sliced mushrooms,
drained
1 teaspoon salt
½ teaspoon pepper
2 tablespoons lemon juice
2 tablespoons parsley flakes

Melt margarine in a skillet or chafing dish. Add tuna; heat and stir about 3 minutes. Remove from heat and stir in remaining ingredients. Cover and cook over low heat, stirring occasionally, until liquid is absorbed (about 10 minutes). Serve hot over bun halves. *Serves 10.*

Tuna Gumbo

1 10½-ounce can chicken gumbo   1 8½-ounce can mixed vegetables,
   soup   drained
1 3¼-ounce can tuna   1 teaspoon catsup

In a saucepan combine soup and tuna; simmer 3 minutes. Add
vegetables and catsup; heat 5 minutes more. Serve hot, with bread
or crackers. *Serves 2.*

Baby Shrimp and Spanish Rice

1 4½-ounce can cooked baby   1 teaspoon lemon juice
  shrimp   2 tablespoons catsup
1 8½-ounce can Spanish rice   Salt and pepper to taste

Drain and rinse shrimp. In a saucepan combine all ingredients
and heat over a low flame about 10 minutes. *Serves 2.*

Sparky Salmon

1 7-ounce can salmon steak   1 teaspoon onion flakes
1 teaspoon lemon juice   1 8½-ounce can stewed tomatoes

Drain salmon and remove skin. Combine salmon, lemon juice,
and onion flakes; mix well. In a saucepan heat tomatoes. Roll
salmon into small balls; place balls on a serving plate and pour
tomatoes over all. *Serves 2.*

Salmon Patties

1 7-ounce can salmon
2 tablespoons mayonnaise

1 teaspoon parsley flakes
2 teaspoons salad oil

Combine all ingredients except salad oil. Shape into patties. In a skillet heat oil. Drop in patties and brown on both sides. Serve hot with rice or your favorite vegetable. *Serves 2.*

Quick Lobster Newburg

1 5-ounce can lobster
1 10½-ounce can cream of celery
  soup
¼ cup water

2 tablespoons powdered milk
1 tablespoon catsup
Salt and pepper to taste

Combine all ingredients and cook over a low flame until hot but not boiling. Serve over toast or rice. *Serves 2.*

Tuna and Macaroni Plus

1 3¼-ounce can tuna
1 16-ounce can macaroni and
  cheese

2 frankfurters, cooked

In a saucepan heat tuna and macaroni and cheese. Slit franks down centers and place on a serving plate. Pour tuna-macaroni mixture over franks. (This combination can also be served over hot buns instead of franks.) *Serves 2.*

Quick Fried Fillets

(To make at home)

1 16-ounce package frozen fish fillets
¼ cup milk

½ cup crushed herb-seasoned
croutons
2 tablespoons margarine

Thaw fillets just enough to separate them. Dip them in milk, then
in croutons. Place in a baking dish greased with margarine. Bake
in a hot 450° oven about 20 minutes. Fish should flake easily
when done. Wrap in foil, refrigerate, and bring to office next day.
To serve, garnish fillets with lemon slices or pour hot tomato
sauce over them. *Serves 4.*

Office Lunch

1 teaspoon lemon juice
Leftover cooked fish
1 tablespoon soy sauce

1 8½-ounce can whole baby
carrots, drained

Spread lemon juice over fish. Combine soy sauce and carrots. Heat
all ingredients in foil on a cooker plate over a low flame about
10 minutes. *Serves 1.*

Salmon Loaf

(To make at home)

1 *pound canned red salmon*   ½ *cup milk*
1 *cup soft bread crumbs*   2 *tablespoons onion flakes*
2 *eggs, well beaten*   1 *tablespoon lemon juice*

Drain salmon; remove skin and bones, then flake. Add remaining ingredients and toss lightly. Place in a greased loaf pan; smooth top. Bake in a 375° oven 40 minutes. Refrigerate covered overnight. Heat when ready to serve, or serve cold. *Serves 4.*

Office Lunch

3 *pitted green olives, sliced*   1 *8½-ounce can stewed tomatoes*
Leftover Salmon Loaf

Press olives into salmon. Place salmon in a saucepan. Add tomatoes and heat over a medium flame about 8 minutes. *Serves 1.*

Salmon and Macaroni

1 *7-ounce can salmon, drained*   ½ *teaspoon prepared mustard*
1 *16-ounce can macaroni and*
  cheese

Flake salmon. In a saucepan combine all ingredients. Heat, stirring often. Serve hot. *Serves 2.*

Sardine Special

1 4-ounce can sardines
1 small tomato, sliced

2 slices American cheese
2 tablespoons bacon bits (optional)

Drain sardines and divide into 2 portions. Place each portion in foil and top with tomato slices; lay cheese slice over each portion. Close foil tightly and heat over a medium flame 5 minutes. Serve from foil with crackers or breadsticks. *Serves 2.*

Quick Herring

1 3¼-ounce can herring fillets or "Kippered snacks"
1 8½-ounce can diced pickled beets

½ cup cottage cheese

Drain herring and beets. Mix beets and cheese; top with herring fillets and serve. *Serves 1.*

Codfish Cakes and Macaroni

4 codfish cakes, canned
1 tablespoon oil

1 16-ounce can macaroni shells in Italian sauce

Slice codfish cakes into 4 serving pieces. In a skillet heat oil and brown cakes on each side. Pour in macaroni and heat about 5 minutes, or until hot. *Serves 2.*

Clam Delight

2 tablespoons oil or margarine
1 8-ounce package frozen clam
   sticks

1 16-ounce can macaroni and
   cheese
1 tablespoon lemon juice

In a skillet heat oil or margarine and brown clam sticks on both sides over a low flame, turning frequently. After 5 minutes, place opened can of macaroni and cheese in skillet and heat through with clam sticks 10 minutes. Arrange clam sticks on a plate, sprinkle with lemon juice, and top with macaroni and cheese. *Serves 2.*

Creamy Herring

1 8-ounce jar herring in cream
   sauce
1 8½-ounce can peas, drained

1 3-ounce can sliced mushrooms,
   drained

Combine all ingredients and serve with crackers or breadsticks, or over toast. *Serves 2.*

Shrimp-a-Roni

1 8½-ounce can macaroni and
   cheese
1 3½-ounce can cooked baby
   shrimp

2 tablespoons catsup
1 teaspoon onion flakes

In a saucepan combine all ingredients. Heat through, stirring occasionally. *Serves 2.*

Tangy Sardines

1 4½-ounce can sardines in tomato
sauce
1 8½-ounce can leaf spinach,
drained

1 tablespoon Parmesan cheese

Combine sardines and spinach and top with Parmesan cheese.
Serves 2.

Shrimp 'n' Beans

1 3½-ounce can cooked baby
shrimp
1 8¼-ounce can Boston baked
beans

½ teaspoon lemon juice

Drain and rinse shrimp. In a saucepan combine shrimp, beans,
and lemon juice. Heat over a low flame about 8 minutes and
serve hot with buns. *Serves 1.*

6

Meat and Poultry

Many meat and poultry dishes are available canned or frozen to make for quick and easy-to-prepare office lunches. Equally handy are cold cuts, which require little or no actual cooking. We've provided several recipes using these convenient foods, with plenty of room for creativity on your part.

For those of you who prefer to display your own finesse rather than rely on frozen or canned meat and poultry courses, we have also included several recipes which, while prepared at your leisure at home, are easily converted into new and tasty dishes during your lunch hour. These "Cook-at-Home" recipes make great dinners and the leftovers equally tasty "Office Lunches." Try these and your luncheon guests will wish they had been at dinner, too!

Corned Beef Skillet Lunch

1 *teaspoon salad oil*
1 *7-ounce can corned beef*
2 *tablespoons catsup*

1 *8¼-ounce can sliced white*
  potatoes, drained

In a skillet heat oil; add corned beef and mix in catsup. Place potatoes on top. Cover and heat 5 minutes. *Serves 2.*

Corned Beef and Sauerkraut

1 *teaspoon salad oil*
1 *7-ounce can corned beef*
1 *packet instant vegetable broth*
  mix

¼ *cup water*
1 *8½-ounce can sauerkraut*

In a skillet heat oil; add corned beef, broth mix, and water. Mash with a fork and place sauerkraut on top. Cover and simmer 10 minutes. *Serves 2.*

Hearty Beef Stew

1 *3¼-ounce can beef stew*
1 *8½-ounce can sliced carrots,*
  drained

1 *8½-ounce can peas, drained*

Place all ingredients in foil. Close foil tightly and place in a skillet. Cover and heat 10 minutes. *Serves 2.*

Chili Con Carne

1 8½-ounce can chili con carne   1 7-ounce can whole-kernel corn

Place ingredients in foil. Close foil tightly and place in a skillet. Cover and heat 10 minutes. Serve over bread or with crackers. *Serves 2.*

Stew with Onions

1 7½-ounce can beef stew
3 tablespoons catsup
1 8½-ounce can whole onions, drained

1 8½-ounce can green peas, drained
1 tablespoon parsley

In a saucepan combine all ingredients except parsley. Heat over a low flame about 10 minutes. Serve hot, topped with parsley. *Serves 4.*

Corned Beef Hash and Spaghetti

1 teaspoon salad oil
1 8-ounce can corned beef hash

1 8½-ounce can spaghetti
1 tablespoon Parmesan cheese

In a skillet heat oil. Brown corned beef hash; add spaghetti and heat about 10 minutes. Serve hot, topped with Parmesan cheese. *Serves 2.*

Corned Beef and Cabbage

1 7-ounce can corned beef
1 tablespoon salad oil

2 tablespoons catsup
1 8½-ounce jar red cabbage

Pierce corned beef with a fork and separate into chunks. In a skillet heat oil; add corned beef and catsup. Mash with fork and heat over a medium flame about 3 minutes. Add cabbage and heat 5 minutes more. *Serves 2.*

Beef and Spanish Rice Dinner

1 2½-ounce jar dried beef
1 15-ounce can Spanish rice dinner

1 teaspoon soy sauce

In a saucepan combine all ingredients; heat until hot. *Serves 2.*

Ravioli Time

1 15-ounce can beef ravioli in
sauce

1 8½-ounce can peas, drained
1 tablespoon Parmesan cheese

In a saucepan heat ravioli; add peas. Serve hot, topped with Parmesan cheese. *Serves 2.*

Pretty Baby Franks

½ cup chili sauce
1 teaspoon lemon juice
1½ teaspoons prepared mustard

3 7-ounce packages cocktail franks
1 8½-ounce can pineapple chunks,
  drained

In a chafing dish combine chili sauce, lemon juice and mustard; add franks and pineapple chunks. Simmer 15 minutes. Serve warm, with toothpicks. *Serves 10.*

Spicy Meatballs

(*To make at home*)

1 16-ounce can spaghetti sauce
2 teaspoons chili powder
1½ pounds ground beef
¼ cup fine dry bread crumbs
3 tablespoons onion flakes

1 teaspoon salt
1 egg, slightly beaten
4 tablespoons margarine
1 small clove garlic, minced
¼ cup water

Mix together half the spaghetti sauce, 1 teaspoon chili powder, beef, bread crumbs, onion flakes, salt, and egg. Shape into small balls about 1 inch in diameter. Brown meatballs in margarine along with garlic and remaining chili powder. Stir in remaining spaghetti sauce and water. Cover and cook over low heat 20 minutes, stirring often. *Makes 30 to 40 meatballs.*

Mini Cheeseburgers

(To make at home)

1½ pounds ground beef
1 teaspoon onion flakes

5 slices American cheese
5 frankfurter rolls

Mix beef and onion flakes in a bowl. Shape into 40 patties 1 inch in diameter; place in a single layer in a shallow baking pan. Bake in a 375° oven 10 minutes. Cut each cheese slice into 9 squares, and place one square over each meat patty. Bake 4 minutes longer, or until cheese melts slightly. Refrigerate overnight. In the office cut each frankfurter roll into fours, to yield 8 pieces each. Place a cheeseburger patty on each piece. Place on a heating tray at 200°. Serve warm. *Makes 40 patties.*

Chinatown Chicken

(To make at home)

10 pounds ready-to-cook broiler-
  fryer, cut into serving pieces
1½ cups flour
1 cup margarine
2 cups catsup

1 cup sherry
½ cup water
½ cup soy sauce
½ cup lemon juice
2 tablespoons brown sugar

Preheat oven to 375°. Coat chicken pieces with flour. In 2 large skillets melt equal portions of margarine. Divide chicken pieces equally and cook until evenly browned; remove to a baking dish. In a saucepan combine catsup, sherry, water, soy sauce, lemon juice, and sugar. Bring to a boil and pour over chicken. Bake covered 1½ hours, or until tender. Refrigerate overnight and serve cold in the office. (For an added zesty flavor, serve with sweet and sour sauce.) *Serves 10.*

Chicken Apple Squares

(To make at home)

2 cups chopped cooked chicken
¼ cup chopped celery
¼ cup margarine
1 tablespoon lemon juice

Salt and pepper to taste
1 *14-ounce jar baked apple rings,*
drained
6 *thin slices bread, crusts removed*

Combine all ingredients except apple rings and bread slices. Cut apple rings and bread slices into quarters. Spread chicken mixture onto bread squares and top with apple-ring quarters. Refrigerate overnight and serve cold in the office. *Makes 24 squares.*

Fruited Ham

1 *slice cooked ham, ½ inch thick,*
or 4 slices luncheon-packed ham

1 *8¼-ounce can sliced pineapple*
rings

Divide ham into 2 portions and place in foil; add pineapple rings with juice. Close foil and heat about 8 minutes. *Serves 2.*

NOTE: Try substituting pineapple with peaches, pears, bananas, cherries, applesauce, or raisins.

Ham Roll-ups

1 teaspoon prepared mustard
4 slices boiled ham

1 8½-ounce can asparagus spears,
  drained

Spread mustard on ham slices; place equal amounts of asparagus in the centers. Roll up and secure with toothpicks. Heat in foil over a medium flame about 3 minutes. *Serves 2.*

Macaroni and Luncheon Meat

1 16-ounce can macaroni and
  cheese
1 cup luncheon meat, diced

2 slices toast
1 teaspoon parsley

In a saucepan heat macaroni and cheese and luncheon meat. Serve hot over toast and top with parsley. *Serves 2.*

Quick Franks and Beans

1 16-ounce can franks and beans in
  tomato sauce

1 teaspoon prepared mustard
1 teaspoon Parmesan cheese

Combine all ingredients and heat in a saucepan, stirring occasionally. Serve as is, or over English muffins. *Serves 2.*

Luncheon Kabobs

1 4-ounce can Vienna sausages
½ 4 fluid-ounce jar pearl onions,
  drained

1 2-ounce jar stuffed olives
2 tablespoons prepared mustard

Cut sausages in half. Spear sausage halves, onions, and olives alternately on toothpicks, with mustard as a dip. *Serves 2.*

Sausage Beans

1 4-ounce can Vienna sausages
1 8½-ounce can baked beans

1 1½-ounce box raisins

Combine all ingredients in foil. Heat over a low flame about 10 minutes. *Serves 2.*

Franks and Corn

1 8½-ounce can cream-style corn
1 teaspoon prepared mustard

2 frankfurters, precooked, cut into
  quarters

Pour corn into a saucepan; stir in mustard. Add franks and cook over a low flame about 5 minutes. *Serves 2.*

Creole Franks

1 8½-ounce can spaghetti sauce
2 frankfurters, precooked

2 frankfurter buns
1 teaspoon onion flakes

In a saucepan heat spaghetti sauce and franks 5 minutes. Add onion flakes. Place franks in buns and spoon sauce over all (can also be served over rice or noodles). *Serves 2.*

Quick Frank Dish

1 16-ounce can spaghetti circles
  with sliced franks in tomato
  sauce

¼ cup dehydrated soup greens
2 tablespoons Parmesan cheese

Place contents of can in a saucepan. Stir in soup greens and heat over a medium flame, stirring occasionally. Serve hot, topped with cheese. *Serves 2.*

Chicken Fricassee

1 16-ounce can chicken fricassee
1 teaspoon soy sauce

1 8½-ounce can asparagus, drained
1 cup cooked rice

In a saucepan heat chicken fricassee in its own gravy, add soy sauce and asparagus. Heat about 10 minutes, stirring often. Serve hot over rice. *Serves 2.*

Beef and Macaroni Casserole

COOK-AT-HOME DINNER

½ cup hot water
1 4-ounce package dried beef
1 10½-ounce can cream of chicken
soup

4 to 6 ounces macaroni
¼ cup shredded cheese

Pour water over dried beef; drain and cut with scissors into
1-inch-long pieces. Add to soup and heat. Boil macaroni accord-
ing to package directions about 10 minutes; drain well. Combine
with beef and soup and pour into 1½-quart casserole. Cover
with cheese. Bake in a moderate 350° oven about 30 minutes.
Serves 4.

OFFICE LUNCH

1 8½-ounce can chopped spinach,
drained
1 teaspoon onion flakes

Leftover Beef and Macaroni Casserole

Combine spinach and onion flakes; place on top of beef and
macaroni in foil. Close foil and heat on a cooker plate over a
medium flame about 8 minutes. *Serves 2.*

Chicken and Mushrooms

COOK-AT-HOME DINNER

1 2¼-pound package quick-frozen
   frying chicken, thawed
2 tablespoons margarine
1 10½-ounce can cream of celery
   soup

1 6-ounce can sliced mushrooms,
   drained

Arrange chicken in a shallow baking dish and dot with margarine. Bake at 400° 20 minutes. Turn chicken; bake 20 minutes more. Stir soup and pour over chicken. Top with mushrooms and bake 20 minutes longer. Stir sauce before serving. *Serves 3 to 4.*

OFFICE LUNCH

½ cup water
½ 1¼-ounce package noodle soup
   mix

Leftover Chicken and Mushrooms
1 8½-ounce can spinach, drained

In a saucepan bring water to a boil; reduce heat and add soup mix. Cover and cook 10 minutes. Add chicken and spinach. Heat 3 minutes more. *Serves 2.*

Veal Parmesan

COOK-AT-HOME DINNER

1 pound veal cutlets
1 egg, slightly beaten
½ cup bread crumbs
2 tablespoons margarine
1 10½-ounce can tomato soup

½ soup can water
½ teaspoon garlic salt
2 ounces mozzarella cheese, thinly
   sliced
2 tablespoons Parmesan cheese

Dip cutlets in egg, then in bread crumbs. Brown in margarine in a skillet. Add soup, water, and garlic salt. Cook over low heat 45 minutes, stirring occasionally. Arrange mozzarella slices on top and sprinkle with Parmesan cheese. Bake in a moderate 350° oven until cheese melts. *Serves 4.*

OFFICE LUNCH

½ cup Leftover Veal Parmesan, diced

1 8½-ounce can whole onions, diced

1 8½-ounce can stewed tomatoes

Salt and pepper to taste

In a saucepan combine all ingredients. Heat over a low flame about 5 minutes. Serve over rice or noodles. *Serves 2.*

Quick Meatballs

COOK-AT-HOME DINNER

1 pound ground beef

¼ cup crushed herb-seasoned croutons

1 egg, slightly beaten

3 tablespoons catsup

1 tablespoon salad oil

Mix beef, croutons, egg, and catsup; shape into small balls. In a skillet brown meatballs in salad oil; pour off drippings. Turn meatballs and cover skillet. Cook over low heat 20 minutes. *Makes about 20 meatballs.*

OFFICE LUNCH

1 8½-ounce can spaghetti

Leftover Quick Meatballs

1 teaspoon Parmesan cheese

Open canned spaghetti; place can on a cooker plate along with meatballs in foil. Heat over a medium flame 10 minutes. Serve meatballs over spaghetti, topped with Parmesan cheese. *Serves 1.*

Minute Steaks

COOK-AT-HOME DINNER

1 teaspoon margarine
2 minute steaks, ¼ inch thick

¼ teaspoon salt

Rub a skillet with margarine and heat. Brown steaks about 2 minutes on each side. Salt to taste. Serve with potatoes and a vegetable or as a sandwich; or serve on toast, topped with gravy or cream sauce. *Serves 1 to 2.*

OFFICE LUNCH

½ 8½-ounce can asparagus tips, drained
Leftover Minute Steak, cut into small pieces

1 teaspoon grated American cheese

Place asparagus tips over steak and top with cheese. Heat on a cooker plate over a medium flame about 5 minutes. *Serves 1.*

Braised Beef and Onions

COOK-AT-HOME DINNER

1 pound round steak
2 tablespoons margarine
1 8½-ounce can small whole onions, drained

1 8½-ounce can stewed tomatoes

Cut beef into strips; brown in margarine in a skillet. Add onions and tomatoes. Cover and cook over low heat 25 minutes, or until meat is tender, stirring occasionally. *Serves 4.*

OFFICE LUNCH
1 8½-ounce can kidney beans   1 teaspoon soy sauce
Leftover Braised Beef and Onions

Place desired amount of beans over beef; add soy sauce. Heat on
a cooker plate over a medium flame 8 minutes. *Serves 1.*

Swedish Meatballs

COOK-AT-HOME DINNER
1 *pound ground beef*   1 *10½-ounce can cream of celery*
¼ *cup crushed herb-seasoned*   *soup*
   croutons   ½ *soup can water*
½ *cup chopped onion*   2 *tablespoons chopped parsley*
1 *egg, slightly beaten*   3 *cups cooked rice*
1 *tablespoon salad oil*

Mix beef, croutons, onion, and egg; shape into small balls. In a
skillet heat oil and brown meatballs; pour off drippings. Stir in
soup and water and top with parsley. Cover and cook over low
heat 20 minutes, stirring often. Serve with rice. *Makes 24 meatballs.*

OFFICE LUNCH
1 *8½-ounce can diced beets,*   *Leftover Swedish Meatballs and*
   drained   *rice*

Open canned beets. Heat meatballs and rice in foil and beets in
can on a cooker plate 5 minutes. Add beets to meatballs and heat
3 more minutes. *Serves 1.*

Corned Beef Hash

COOK-AT-HOME DINNER

1 *8-ounce can corned beef hash*
1 *tablespoon onion flakes*
1 *7-ounce can whole-kernel corn*

2 *tablespoons catsup*
1 *tablespoon margarine*

Combine all ingredients and place in a greased casserole or pie pan, spreading evenly. Bake in a moderate 350° oven 20 to 25 minutes. *Serves 2.*

OFFICE LUNCH

1 *peach, halved*
Leftover Corned Beef Hash
¼ *cup peach syrup*

1 *teaspoon brown sugar or cinnamon*

Pack each peach half with corned beef hash; place in foil. Pour syrup over all and top with brown sugar or cinnamon. Close foil tightly and heat on a cooker plate over a low flame about 8 minutes. *Serves 1.*

Broiled Ham Steak

COOK-AT-HOME DINNER

¾ *pound ready-to-eat ham steak*
  (1 *inch thick*)
2 *tablespoons prepared mustard*

2 *tablespoons brown sugar*
1 *tablespoon orange juice*

Slash fat along edges of steak to prevent ham from curling. Place ham in foil and broil 3 inches from heat about 5 minutes. Turn and spread with mustard, sugar, and juice. Broil 5 minutes longer (top should be glazed). *Serves 2.*

1 3¼-ounce can tuna   2 tablespoons soy sauce
Leftover Broiled Ham Steak, diced

Drain and flake tuna; combine with ham and soy sauce. Wrap tightly in foil and heat on a cooker plate over a medium flame 5 minutes. *Serves 1.*

No-Cook Ham Loaf

COOK-AT-HOME DINNER
1 tablespoon unflavored gelatin   2 tablespoons lemon juice
¼ cup cold water   2 teaspoons onion flakes
1 cup boiling water   2 cups finely chopped cooked ham

Dissolve gelatin in cold water. Add boiling water and chill until slightly thickened. Stir in ham, lemon juice, and onion flakes; pour into a small loaf pan or mold and chill until firm. Unmold, slice, and serve cold. *Serves 4.*

OFFICE LUNCH
1 tablespoon relish   1 slice Swiss cheese
Leftover No-Cook Ham Loaf   4 green olives, sliced

Spread relish on ham loaf in foil; top with cheese and olives. Close foil tightly and heat on a cooker plate over a medium flame 5 minutes. Open foil and heat 3 minutes more. *Serves 1.*

Stuffed Peppers

COOK-AT-HOME DINNER

½ pound ground beef
1 cup cooked rice
1 tablespoon onion flakes

1 10½-ounce can tomato soup
4 medium green peppers
¼ cup water

Combine beef, rice, onion flakes, and ¼ cup soup. Cut off a 1-inch piece from the stem end of each pepper; carefully remove seeds and fibers. Rinse peppers and stuff with meat mixture. Arrange peppers upright in a saucepan; pour in remaining soup and water. Cover and cook over low heat 1 hour, adding a little water if sauce gets too thick.

Or

Stuff peppers as described above. Place in a 1½-quart casserole and bake in a 375° oven 30 minutes. Heat remaining soup and pour over peppers. *Serves 4.*

OFFICE LUNCH

1 8½-ounce can zucchini
Leftover Stuffed Pepper

4 pitted black olives

Open canned zucchini. Heat pepper in foil and zucchini in can on a cooker plate over a low flame 15 minutes. Pour zucchini over pepper and top with olives. *Serves 1.*

All-Purpose Meat Loaf

COOK-AT-HOME DINNER

1 16-ounce can spaghetti sauce
1 cup crushed herb-seasoned
   croutons
1 egg, slightly beaten

¼ teaspoon pepper
¼ cup water
1½ pounds ground beef

In a large bowl combine sauce, croutons, egg, pepper, and water. Add beef and mix all ingredients thoroughly. Shape firmly into a loaf and place in a shallow 12 × 8 × 2-inch baking pan. Bake in a 350° oven 1¼ hours. *Serves 6.*

OFFICE LUNCH

1 15-ounce packet instant beef
  broth mix
¼ cup water
Leftover All-Purpose Meat Loaf

1 8½-ounce can sliced potatoes,
  drained
1 teaspoon onion flakes

In a saucepan dissolve broth mix in water; bring to a boil. Add meat loaf and potatoes; top with onion flakes. Heat 5 minutes. *Serves 1.*

Pepper Steak

COOK-AT-HOME DINNER

1 pound round steak
2 tablespoons margarine
1 16-ounce can spaghetti sauce

1 small green pepper, cut into
  1-inch-thick pieces

Pound steak with a hammer or the edge of a heavy saucer. In a skillet brown meat in margarine; pour off fat. Stir in spaghetti sauce. Cover and cook over low heat 30 minutes. Add pepper and cook uncovered 30 minutes more, stirring often. *Serves 4.*

OFFICE LUNCH

½ 13½-ounce can Chinese rice
Leftover Pepper Steak

1 teaspoon soy sauce

Combine rice, steak, and soy sauce in a saucepan. Heat over a low flame 10 minutes, stirring often. *Serves 1.*

Swiss Steak and Vegetables

COOK-AT-HOME DINNER

¼ cup flour
1½ pounds round steak
2 tablespoons margarine
1 10½-ounce can tomato soup
Soup can water
Salt and pepper to taste

1 tablespoon onion flakes
1 16-ounce can sliced carrots, drained
1 16-ounce can baby round potatoes, drained

Pound flour into steak with a meat hammer or the edge of a heavy saucer. Cut meat into 4 serving pieces. In a large skillet brown steak on both sides in margarine; add soup, water, and salt and pepper. Cover and cook over low heat 45 minutes; add carrots, potatoes, and onion flakes and heat 10 minutes more. When serving, spoon pan liquid over all. *Serves 4.*

OFFICE LUNCH

If leftover portion contains both steak and vegetables, wrap it in foil and heat 7 minutes. If only the meat is left, try it this way:

1 8½-ounce can tomato sauce
Leftover Swiss Steak
2 slices bread

Open canned tomato sauce and heat in can on a cooker plate over a medium flame 5 minutes. Place steak between bread slices and pour on tomato sauce. *Serves 1.*

Top-of-the-Stove Chicken

COOK-AT-HOME DINNER

1 2-pound chicken, cut into serving pieces
¼ cup flour
¼ cup margarine

½ soup can water
1 10½-ounce can tomato soup
Salt and pepper to taste

Coat chicken pieces with flour; brown in margarine in a skillet. Stir in water and soup and add salt and pepper to taste. Cover and simmer 45 minutes, or until chicken is tender, stirring often. *Serves 4.*

OFFICE LUNCH

Leftover Top-of-the-Stove Chicken	*1 small tomato, sliced*
2 lettuce leaves	*Potato chips*

Make a cold platter of chicken, lettuce, and tomato, surrounded by potato chips. *Serves 1.*

Honey-Glazed Chicken

COOK-AT-HOME DINNER

2 broiler-fryers, cut into serving pieces	*1/4 cup honey*
1 tablespoon steak sauce	*1/4 cup orange juice*

Arrange chicken pieces in a single layer in a shallow roasting pan. Combine remaining ingredients and brush generously over chicken. Bake in a 400° oven 40 to 50 minutes, or until tender. *Serves 4.*

OFFICE LUNCH

1/2 8 1/2-ounce can yams or sweet potatoes in syrup	*1 teaspoon soy sauce*
Leftover Honey-Glazed Chicken, diced	

In a skillet heat yams or sweet potatoes in syrup 5 minutes; stir in soy sauce. Add chicken and heat 5 minutes more. Serve hot with a muffin or roll. *Serves 1.*

Chicken Breasts and Sliced Apples

COOK-AT-HOME DINNER

¼ cup margarine	Salt and pepper to taste
4 large chicken breasts	1 chicken bouillon cube
1 onion, sliced	1 cup hot water
2 tablespoons flour	1 14-ounce can sliced apple rings

In a large skillet melt margarine. Sauté chicken breasts on both sides until browned. Add onion and cook 5 minutes. In a small bowl combine flour and salt and pepper; slowly stir in bouillon cube dissolved in hot water. Pour mixture over chicken and cook slowly, covered, 25 minutes, or until chicken is tender. Place apple rings on top of chicken and cook 10 minutes more. (Be sure to reserve enough chicken for Office Lunch.) *Serves 4.*

OFFICE LUNCH

Leftover Chicken Breasts	1 8-ounce can macaroni and cheese

Combine ingredients in a saucepan and heat over a medium flame about 5 minutes. Serve hot as is, or over toast. *Serves 1.*

7

Vegetables and Salads

VEGETABLES

Vegetables and salads are always in style. Leafy green or yellow vegetables are rich in vitamins and a powerful aid to your daily nutrition. Plan to have a serving of each twice a day.

Canned Vegetables—The biggest convenience of canned vegetables is that you can heat and eat them directly from the cans. Combine them with each other for a zesty change of pace; the variety of combinations is virtually endless. For added flavor stir in a teaspoon of soy sauce, catsup, or mayonnaise or try a cheese topping.

Frozen Vegetables—When buying frozen vegetables check the cooking time on the package. It should not be more than 10 minutes—less if possible. Frozen food packages can be cut in half, enabling you to bring to the office only the portion to be used. However, it's sometimes better to cook the entire contents of the package and save the remaining portion for the next day's lunch; this way you are that much ahead in your menu schedule. Always follow manufacturers' instructions for cooking.

Cooking in a Bag—Most frozen vegetables come in plastic bags that are simply dropped in boiling water. Cooking time starts when the water comes to a second boil. When the vegetable in sauce is completely cooked, just cut open the plastic bag and pour the contents over your main course. Of course, these vegetables in sauce are delicious by themselves.

French-fried Potatoes

The only way to have really crisp French fries is to cook them in deep fat in a skillet; this is not recommended for office cooking. However, you don't have to do without them—splurge and order in this treat, or do it this way:

Sprinkle skillet with salt before heating oil; this will help prevent spattering. Heat oil and add a few frozen potatoes at a time. Cook until golden brown (about 5 minutes). Drain on a napkin or paper towel; season to taste.

Mashed Potatoes

½ cup water
Dash salt

¼ cup milk
½ cup potato flakes

Pour water and salt into a saucepan and bring to a boil. Remove from heat and immediately add milk. Add potato flakes and stir gently until flakes are soft and moist. Whip to desired consistency and season to taste. (For softer potatoes add more milk; for firmer potatoes, add more potato flakes.) *Serves 2.*

Potato Pancakes

¼ cup oil   1 1-pound can potato pancakes

In a skillet heat oil; open can at both ends and use one end as a plunger to push out pancake loaf. Cut 4 firm, even slices by using rim of can as a guide. When oil is hot, fry each slice until golden brown on both sides. Season to taste. *Serves 4.*

Hashed Browns

1 cup water   1½ tablespoons salad oil or
½ 5½-ounce package hashed   margarine
   brown potatoes   1 teaspoon salt

Pour water in a skillet; add potatoes and margarine. Cook uncovered over medium-high heat until liquid is absorbed and potatoes are brown on one side (about 8 to 10 minutes). Turn with a spatula, adding salt, and brown on other side (about 3 minutes). *Serves 2.*

Broiled Tomatoes

2 ripe tomatoes, cut in half   2 tablespoons bacon chips or 2
1 tablespoon Parmesan cheese   slices precooked bacon, crumbled

Place tomatoes, cut sides down, in foil; heat over a low flame on a cooker plate 5 minutes. Turn and top with cheese and bacon chips or crumbled bacon. Heat 5 minutes more. *Serves 2.*

Stuffed Tomatoes

Keep tomatoes refrigerated until ready to use. Allow one tomato for each serving. Cut off ¼- to ½-inch slice from stem end; with a teaspoon scoop out pulp and discard. Fill with your favorite stuffing (tuna salad, egg salad, macaroni salad, etc.).

Instant Rice

⅓ cup water
Dash salt

⅓ cup quick-cooking rice

Bring water and salt to a boil; stir in rice. Cover and remove from heat; let stand 5 minutes. Fluff with a fork. *Yields ⅔ cup.*

Cook-at-Home Rice

2½ cups water
1 cup rice

1 teaspoon salt

Bring water to a boil; add rice and salt. Cover tightly and cook over low heat until all water is absorbed (about 25 minutes). (For firmer rice, use less water; for softer rice, use more water.) *Yields 4 cups.*

Raisin Rice

⅓ cup water
Dash salt

1 1½-ounce box raisins
⅓ cup quick-cooking rice

In a saucepan bring water to a boil; add salt and raisins and stir in rice. Cover and remove from heat; let stand 5 minutes. Serve hot. *Serves 2.*

Spanish Rice

½ 7½-ounce package quick-
  cooking Spanish rice
1 tablespoon margarine
2 cups hot water

½ envelope seasonings (enclosed
  in package)
1 16-ounce can diced tomatoes

In a skillet brown rice in margarine until light brown, stirring frequently. Slowly pour in water and stir in seasonings. Add tomatoes; stir and bring to a boil. Cover pan and simmer until liquid is absorbed and rice is tender (about 15 minutes). Sprinkle with grated cheese if desired. *Serves 2.*

Mexicali Rice

½ 7-ounce package cheese-flavored rice
1 tablespoon margarine
1½ cups hot water
½ envelope cheese sauce (enclosed in package)

1 7-ounce can whole-kernel corn, drained
½ cup cottage cheese

In a skillet brown rice in margarine until light brown, stirring frequently. Slowly pour in water and corn. Cover and simmer 15 minutes; do not drain. Stir in cheese sauce and cook 1 minute more until blended. Fold in cottage cheese. *Serves 2.*

Browned Rice

1 tablespoon margarine
¾ cup quick-cooking rice

¼ teaspoon salt
¾ cup bouillon

Melt margarine in a saucepan. Add rice and sauté over medium heat until golden brown, stirring constantly; add salt and bouillon. Bring quickly to a boil. Cover and remove from heat; let stand 5 minutes. Fluff with a fork. *Serves 2.*

Hawaiian Rice

1⅓ cups water
1 15¼-ounce can pineapple tidbits
¼ cup brown sugar

½ teaspoon salt
2 tablespoons margarine
1⅓ cups quick-cooking rice

Bring all ingredients, except rice, to a boil in a saucepan. Add rice. Cover and simmer 10 minutes. *Serves 4.*

Chickeny Fried Rice

1 13½-ounce can fried rice with
   chicken

1 teaspoon soy sauce
1 tablespoon onion flakes

In a saucepan combine all ingredients. Heat over a low flame about 8 minutes, stirring frequently. *Serves 2.*

Beef Fried Rice with Nuts

4 tablespoons margarine
2 8-ounce packages beef-flavored
   quick-cooking rice

5½ cups hot water
½ cup salted peanuts

In large deep pan, heat margarine. Add contents of both packages of rice. (Set aside the small envelope that's inserted in package.) Stir rice frequently until lightly browned. Pour slowly into browned rice 5½ cups hot water. Stir in contents of both envelopes of beef flavoring. Cover and simmer until liquid is absorbed and rice is tender, about 15 to 18 minutes. When done, transfer to serving dish and top with peanuts. *Serves 10.*

SALADS

Salads, both hot and cold, are light and lively and easy to prepare. Salad greens help spark up the flavor and appearance of any basic salad. Lettuce, celery, and raw cabbage are among the most popular on the restaurant menus. Serve any of these delicious salads on a lettuce leaf, add shredded carrot, black or green olives, chopped pepper, green onion, or celery. Seasoned salts and mixed salad herbs come in shakers that are easy to store and last about 6 months. Bacon-flavored bits, vinegar, lemon juice, curry powder, or mayonnaise also work wonders for your salad.

Cottage cheese is one of the most versatile salad foods; it seems to go with everything. Serve it with fruit, cheese, vegetables, meat, fish, or poultry.

Relishes and salad dressings satisfy our desire for something "extra" and perk up the blandest of salads. Cucumbers, dill pickles, sweet and sour pickles, cherry tomatoes, pickled cabbage, beans, onions, chili sauce, and catsup are among the many choices available.

Bottled and packaged dressings also enhance the taste of salads immeasurably. Popular choices are blue cheese, Caesar, French, garlic, Italian, oil and vinegar, onion, Parmesan cheese, Roquefort, Russian, and Thousand Islands.

Tuna Fish Salad

1 3¼-ounce can tuna fish
2 tablespoons mayonnaise

1 teaspoon parsley flakes
1 lettuce leaf

Drain oil from tuna; place in a cup or bowl. Mix in mayonnaise and parsley flakes thoroughly. Spoon onto lettuce leaf. *Serves 1.*

Beef Salad

½ cup macaroni salad
1 3-ounce package smoked corned
   beef

1 teaspoon dry mustard

Place half of the macaroni salad on a plate. Arrange half of the corned beef over it; spread mustard over beef. Top with remaining salad and beef and serve. (Bologna, ham, or any of the luncheon meats can be substituted for corned beef.) *Serves 1.*

Chicken Salad

1 5-ounce can boned chicken
2 tablespoons French dressing

1/4 cup chopped celery

Drain chicken. In a cup or bowl combine chicken with dressing and celery. Mix well and serve. *Serves 1.*

Ham Salad

1 lettuce leaf
1 small tomato, sliced

1/2 cup diced ham
2 tablespoons mayonnaise

Place lettuce leaf on a plate; arrange tomato slices around edges. Mix ham and mayonnaise and spoon equal portions onto each tomato slice. *Serves 1.*

Coleslaw

1/4 head green or red cabbage,
    shredded
2 tablespoons mayonnaise

1 teaspoon lemon juice or dry
    mustard

Combine all ingredients and mix thoroughly.

NOTE: Try the following additions to dress up your basic coleslaw: pears, diced apples, pineapple chunks, cranberry gelatin, your favorite canned vegetables, prunes, dates, raisins, or hard-cooked eggs. *Serves 2.*

Fiesta Salad

1 teaspoon margarine
½ cup chopped cabbage
1 8½-ounce can kidney beans in
    sauce

1 16-ounce can Spanish rice

In a skillet heat margarine and cook cabbage about 3 minutes;
add beans and rice. Heat over a medium flame about 5 minutes
and serve hot. *Serves 2.*

Lemon Fruit Cocktail

1 8¾-ounce can fruit cocktail
1 teaspoon lemon juice

1 lettuce leaf
1 teaspoon cinnamon

In a saucepan heat fruit cocktail and lemon juice. Serve hot over
lettuce leaf; top with cinnamon. *Serves 1.*

Sauerkraut Salad

1 16-ounce can sauerkraut
6 stuffed green olives

1 8½-ounce jar beet and garden
    salad, drained

Combine all ingredients in foil and heat on a cooker plate about
10 minutes. Serve hot with rolls. *Serves 2.*

Chinese Salad

1 16-ounce can mixed Chinese
 vegetables
1 tablespoon soy sauce

1 7-ounce can boned chicken
2 lettuce leaves

Drain off half the liquid from vegetables; pour remaining half with vegetables into a saucepan. Add soy sauce and chicken. Heat about 8 minutes. Spoon equal portions onto each lettuce leaf. *Serves 2.*

Crabmeat Delight

1 7¾-ounce can crabmeat
1 lettuce leaf, shredded

1 8½-ounce can stewed tomatoes
½ cup chopped celery

Combine all ingredients and heat over a medium flame about 5 minutes. *Serves 2.*

EXTRA-QUICK SALADS

The "deli" or commercially prepared salads make great side dishes. Add one of your favorite meats and you have a main course. Purchased by the pound or fraction of a pound, these products are quite economical and tasty.

Mini Chef Salad

2 slices Swiss cheese
1 3-ounce slice smoked turkey

2 slices ham or tongue
½ pound mixed green salad

Cut cheese and meats into thin strips and toss with salad. Add your favorite dressing and serve. *Serves 2.*

German-style Potato Salad

½ pound German-style potato
  salad
1 hard-cooked egg, crumbled

1 dill pickle, thinly sliced
1 teaspoon parsley flakes
1 teaspoon mayonnaise

Combine all ingredients and mix well. *Serves 1.*

Italian Salad Roll-ups

2 slices American cheese
2 slices salami

½ pound Italian salad

Place one slice cheese on each slice salami. Divide salad in half
and place in center of each cheese slice. Roll up and secure with
toothpicks. *Serves 2.*

Chopped Liver Salad

2 lettuce leaves
½ pound chopped liver

4 green olives, sliced
½ pound beet salad

Place a lettuce leaf on each serving plate. Place equal portions of
liver in center of each plate; top with olives. Spoon beet salad
around edges and serve. *Serves 2.*

8

Desserts

What is a meal without dessert? Desserts round out our menus and give us that "something sweet" that we all crave. With a few exceptions, any dessert can be yours for the preparing in the office. Try these delicious, easy-to-do recipes that give you the most for the least amount of money.

PUDDINGS

Life gets easier all the time. For example, we now have puddings in cans with zip-open tops that eliminate the need of a can opener. Just lift the ring to the edge of the can, pull up to remove the entire top, and eat right out of the can. They taste just like homemade puddings without all the bother; they are packaged four to a carton and cost about fifteen cents per five-ounce serving. The most popular flavor offerings are chocolate, vanilla, lemon, and caramel.

Deluxe Vanilla Pudding

1 5-ounce can vanilla pudding   ½ 1½-ounce box raisins

Open pudding and mix in raisins. Place can on a cooker plate and heat over a medium flame until hot. *Serves 1.*

Hot Nutty Chocolate Pudding

1 5-ounce can chocolate pudding   1 tablespoon crushed peanuts

Open pudding and place can on a cooker plate. Heat over a medium flame until hot. Top with peanuts and serve. *Serves 1.*

Caramel Dessert Shell

1 5-ounce can caramel pudding   1 dessert shell

Open pudding and place on a cooker plate. Heat over a medium flame until hot. Pour pudding into dessert shell and serve hot. *Serves 1.*

Fruited Lemon Pudding

1 5-ounce can lemon pudding   1 8¾-ounce can fruit cocktail, drained

Open cans and place on a cooker plate. Heat over a medium flame until hot. Pour fruit into a serving dish and top with pudding. *Serves 1.*

SOME LIKE IT COLD!

Canned puddings cool quickly when refrigerated. For a creamy and different taste, try these combinations:
- To 1 can cold vanilla pudding add 2 tablespoons maraschino cherries.
- To 1 can cold chocolate pudding add 2 tablespoons shredded coconut.
- To 1 can cold caramel pudding add 2 tablespoons miniature marshmallows.
- To 1 can cold lemon pudding add 1 tablespoon cinnamon.

NO-COOK INSTANT GELATINS

You're in for a real treat with these handy prejelled products. These desserts are packaged in lightweight plastic cups with foil-covered tops that peel right off. Just chill for thirty minutes and they're ready to eat—right from the cup. There are four four-fluid-ounce servings to a carton, and strawberry, lemon, lime, and raspberry are among the flavors you'll enjoy. Serve them as is or with canned or fresh fruit. For a tasty variation, place the gelatin mold in a dessert shell and top with one of the canned puddings.

CAKES

Packaged cake has long been one of our most cherished institutions—and no wonder, for their convenience is hard to beat. These tasty time-savers should be high on your list of staples for the Office Cook-in Plan.

On "rush" days, packaged ready-to-eat goodies for two come readily to your aid. Doughnuts—sugared, plain, jellied, or chocolate-covered—make delightfully different desserts. Cupcakes, Danish, tarts, and the vast assortment of cookies available help greatly to satisfy the sweet side of life.

There will be days, however, when you'll feel really ambitious and want to add a touch of your own. No one has the time to bake a cake in the office, even with the quickest cake mix—but the basic packaged pound cake can be the start of something special! Try it toasted with cinnamon; or use any of the following toppings:
- Hot honey or pancake syrup
- Jellies and jams
- Peanut butter
- Hot fruits
- Puddings
- Whipped cream
- Hot sauces

And raisin pound cake is a dessert in itself.

You can even make a layer cake with plain pound cake; try the recipes on page 113.

Apple Stack Cake

2 *canned sliced apples*   2 *slices pound cake*

Cut pound cake slices in half. Starting with cake half, make alternate layers of apple slices and cake. Top with remaining apple slices and syrup from can. *Serves 1.*

Chocolate Layer Cake

2 *slices pound cake*   8 *tablespoons ready-to-eat*
                                             chocolate frosting

Cut pound cake slices in half; spread frosting on each piece. Stack cake halves one on top of the other and coat sides with remaining frosting. *Serves 1.*

Strawberry Long Cake

2 *slices pound cake*   2 *tablespoons canned vanilla*
1 *8¾-ounce can strawberries in*   *whipped-cream frosting*
  syrup

Cover 1 slice pound cake with half of the strawberries; spread on enough whipped cream to cover. Place second cake slice over that and top with remaining strawberries, cream, and syrup from can. *Serves 1.*

ICE CREAM

If you are an ice-cream-for-dessert fan, plan to indulge yourself after dinner. Ice cream *must* be kept frozen and cannot be wrapped and brought to the office. However, if the ice cream urge gets to be so strong that dinnertime seems to be a century away, by all means include it in your menu—after your lunch-in go for a walk, and on your way stop at a soda fountain and eat it there. Your plain old ice-cream-in-a-dish may suddenly become a real treat.

WHIPPED CREAM

Whipped cream makes any dessert glamorous and inviting. Since this is a refrigerated item, it should not be left at room temperature for long periods of time. When bringing it to the office, pack it with freezer cans and refrigerate immediately. Buy only the amount you plan to use within a two-week period; it's not advisable to store it longer than that. Canned whipped cream is sweeter and not so light in texture and taste as the cold variety. After using the former, cover the unused portion with foil and refrigerate.

PIES

Individual pie servings are available in a wide assortment of flavors: blueberry, apple, lemon, cherry, and pineapple, to name only a few. They are quite economical and tasty. Serve as is, or add a topping of whipped cream or sauce. To heat pies wrap them in foil and place on a cooker plate over a low flame for five minutes.

FRUITS

Fruit is a many-splendored thing. Whether it be fresh or canned, plan to have it often during your office lunch-ins. An apple, orange, or can of fruit in your desk drawer can be a great morale supporter in your plan to save money by preparing lunches yourself. Whenever between-meal hunger pangs come on the scene or the coffee wagon gets ominously close to your desk, simply reach out for the fruit—you'll be glad you did. And of course, fruit, whether by itself or topped with syrup, spices, honey, or whipped cream, makes economical and delicious desserts. Just keep one thing in mind. Fresh fruit should always be washed thoroughly before eating.

Hawaiian Melon

1 *ripe honeydew melon or cantaloupe*

1 *8½-ounce can crushed pineapple, drained*

Cut melon in half, scoop out center to remove all seeds. (Wrap seeds in a paper towel and discard immediately; they tend to give off a strong odor.) Place equal portions of crushed pineapple into each melon center and serve. Top with whipped cream if desired. *Serves 2.*

Honey Banana

2 *ripe bananas*   4 *tablespoons honey or syrup*

Peel bananas and cut into 1-inch-long chunks. Wrap in foil and pour honey or syrup over them. Heat on a cooker plate over a medium flame about 5 minutes. Serve hot, with toothpicks. *Serves 2.*

Peach Cup

2 *large peaches*   1 *1½-ounce box raisins*
1 *5-ounce can caramel pudding*

Cut peaches in half and scoop out centers. Spoon pudding into center of each peach half; top with raisins.

NOTE: Canned peach halves can be used instead of the fresh variety. Discard the syrup, or save and use as a topping for another dessert the next day. *Serves 2.*

Purple Plum Compote

1 *8¾-ounce can purple plums with*   1 *8½-ounce can sour cherries with*
   syrup   *syrup*
Syrup from 8½-ounce can peaches
   or apricots

Drain all syrups from cans into a saucepan; cook over medium heat 5 minutes, stirring constantly. Pour syrup over plums and cherries. *Serves 2.*

Cherry Fruit Combo

1 8¾-ounce can fruit cocktail   1 teaspoon cinnamon
1 8½-ounce can cherries, drained

In a saucepan combine fruit cocktail and cherries. Heat over a low flame 5 minutes. Serve hot, sprinkled with cinnamon. *Serves 2.*

Grapy Grapefruit Dessert

1 8½-ounce can grapefruit   1 cup green seedless grapes, chilled
    sections, chilled   1 teaspoon brown sugar

Arrange grapefruit sections around the edge of a saucer or serving plate; reserve syrup. Place grapes in center of plate, sprinkle with sugar, and pour syrup over all. *Serves 2.*

Baked Apples

1 21-ounce can baked apples   2 tablespoons whipped cream or
1 teaspoon cinnamon   marshmallows

Open canned apples; place can on a cooker plate over medium heat about 8 minutes. Pour apples onto serving plates and top with cinnamon and whipped cream or marshmallows. *Serves 2.*

Apple Rings and Bacon

1 14½-ounce can apple rings,
   drained

2 slices bacon, precooked
½ teaspoon sugar

In foil place alternate layers of apple rings and bacon; heat in a saucepan 5 minutes. Sprinkle with sugar and serve with toast. *Serves 1.*

Suggested Fruit Combos

Try any of these combinations for interesting and tasty desserts; add a topping, or heat syrups in cans and pour over fruit.
    Pineapple rings and cherries
    Orange wedges and cantaloupe balls
    Peaches and plums
    Apricots and peaches
    Thinly sliced bananas and cranberry sauce
    Fruit cocktail and dates

WAFFLES

For a change of taste, the frozen waffle (which you just heat in the toaster) can be a base for any of the recipes in this chapter. Wrap the waffle in foil and refrigerate as soon as you get to the office. At lunchtime heat in foil on a cooker plate. To toast, pierce a fork in center of waffle and hold 2 inches from flame; turn and toast other side. Top with syrup, fruit, whipped cream, custard, or any other of your dessert favorites.

9

Beverages

Beverages are costly items whether you buy them in a restaurant or from the coffee wagon. The carbonated drinks are usually diluted, and the coffee may be too strong or the tea water not hot enough, which tends to make you throw away as much as you consume. Individual servings of such other choices as orange, tomato, or grapefruit juice cost three times as much as you would pay for a six-pack of the same size cans from your local grocer. A small jar or can of chocolate syrup can make enough hot chocolate drinks for two weeks, plus you get double value when you use it as a topping for desserts. The cost for this item is equivalent to that of two hot chocolate drinks from the counter.

THE WORLD OF INSTANT DRINKS

"Instant," "fast," "immediate," "hurry," "rush" are the key words for today's living, and the food manufacturer has to tool up to keep pace with it all. Instant beverage mixes are one of the results. Just add water, hot or cold, and the drink of your choice is ready.

The prepared mixes come in many fruit flavors to satisfy your thirst for variety. Try mixing and matching, or add ginger ale or club soda instead of water.

Instant dry milk mix is another choice and a convenient way to get extra nourishment. To 1 glass cold water add 3½ tablespoons mix; stir until smooth. Serve cold, or heat and mix with chocolate syrup or mix to make the ever popular hot chocolate.

Try the following recipes and *vive la différence!*

Rooty Root Beer

3 teaspoons root beer mix
½ glass cold water

1 teaspoon chocolate syrup or mix
3 ice cubes

Pour root beer mix into a glass; add water and chocolate syrup or mix and stir well. Add ice cubes; stir again and serve. *Serves 1.*

Creamy Root Beer Drink

3 teaspoons root beer mix
½ glass cold water
2 ice cubes

2 tablespoons canned vanilla
  pudding

Pour mix into a glass; add water and stir well. Add pudding and ice cubes; stir quickly 10 seconds. *Serves 1.*

Coffee Root Beer

1 cup water
1 tablespoon root beer mix

1 rounded tablespoon instant
  coffee

In a saucepan boil water. In a serving cup mix root beer and coffee together. Add boiling water; stir. Add sugar and cream if desired, or serve it black.

NOTE: For cold coffee root beer dilute root beer mix as directed on package; pour into an ice cube tray and freeze. At serving time make hot instant coffee and add 3 to 4 ice cubes. *Serves 1.*

Orange Tea

1 *teaspoon orange juice mix*   1 *cup hot tea*

Dissolve mix in tea and stir well. No lemon, cream, or sugar needed. *Serves 1.*

Hawaiian Iced Tea

3 *teaspoons iced tea mix*   ½ *cup pineapple juice*
½ *glass cold water*   *Ice cubes*

Dissolve mix in water and stir. Add juice and ice cubes and stir thoroughly. *Serves 1.*

Milk Fizz

3½ *tablespoons instant milk mix*   ½ *cup your favorite carbonated*
½ *glass cold water*   *drink*

Add mix to water and stir well. Add carbonated drink, stirring quickly until bubbles form on top. *Serves 1.*

10

A Message to Dieters

A SENSIBLE APPROACH
TO SUCCESSFUL DIETING

There are a thousand and one diet formulas—but most will work only for a brief period of time. Many diet plans fail basically because the dieter drops the diet! Why does this happen? The answer is simply that the particular diet isn't right for him, and therefore the dieter tires of doing something that is too difficult and not sensible. Very few of us want to cut out bread, meat, butter, or cakes and other desserts for an indefinite period. Still fewer of us want to drink eight glasses of water daily or become vegetarians.

The truly successful dieter is one who eats a wide variety of foods in moderation. True, there are certain foods to be avoided or, if consumed, they should be balanced with other foods. The secret to sensible dieting is to outthink your stomach!

Foods are classified into three categories: protein, carbohydrates, and fats. A favorable daily intake would be: 15 percent protein, 65 percent carbohydrates, and 20 percent fats. Diet-minded individuals should remember that excess protein speeds up weight reduction and carbohydrates and fats slow it down—fats being the worst offenders. Therefore, to maintain your current weight eat a balanced diet; to lose weight cut down on high-calorie carbohydrates and fats and increase your protein consumption.

THE DIET PROBLEM

Fatty and high-carbohydrate foods are usually the tastiest and the easiest to become addicted to. If we could learn to eat them in moderation we wouldn't have a weight problem in the first place. So a successful diet is not one that merely enables us to lose weight but one that trains us to eat a variety of foods in moderation.

As a follower of the Office Cook-in Plan you will learn one of the most important diet techniques: Bring and prepare only the portion to be eaten that day! You don't want to have leftovers in the office—if there are no leftovers you can't eat them! You won't need or want them if you arrange a filling and satisfying menu to enjoy at lunchtime. Try to fit in a first course, an entree, and a beverage—something to take the edge off your appetite. Make a mental note (to your stomach) to always leave room for dessert; there are many low-calorie fruits, puddings, and gelatins available. Ice milk instead of ice cream can do the job of satisfying your sweet tooth nutritiously, at the same time helping you avoid overeating.

THE URGE FIGHTERS

Low-sugar beverages, water, seltzer, coffee, tea, soups
Melba toast, crackers, breadsticks
Gum
Ice milk, yogurt
Low-calorie gelatins, puddings, fresh fruit
Low-calorie cookies, candies
Raw vegetables (carrots, lettuce, radishes, etc.)

PROTEIN: THE "FAT KILLER"

Eggs—poached, hard-boiled, fried (without butter), omelets

Meats and fish—Avoid hamburger patties unless broiled. Trim all fat off meat and broil, bake, or roast—do not fry.

Milk and cheese—Skim milk has the protein without the fat content. Farmer or cottage cheese can do much to aid your weight-loss program.

TIPS FOR LOSING WEIGHT

1. Do not skip meals. Eat your three complete meals at the right time each day.

2. Eat nothing between meals except fresh fruits and perhaps a bedtime snack of a glass of skim milk.

3. Hot beverages such as coffee and tea should be consumed without cream; use lemon with tea. One teaspoon sugar, carefully measured, may be added to a cup of coffee or tea in the morning or afternoon.

4. Don't drink large amounts of water at mealtime, or for one hour before or after your meal.

5. Use a minimum of salt, as it is known to promote the retention of water in the body tissues.

6. Stay away from cake, cookies, and pastries—they have no place in a diet program.

7. Weigh yourself once every week, using the same scale, wearing the same weight apparel, and at the same time of day.

8. Be patient and do not despair. Your reduction in weight will be gradual but it will be definite if you do not cheat. Often the first week's loss of fat will be replaced in your body with water.

9. Supplement your diet with a multivitamin capsule.

10. See your family physician regularly for a checkup. If you should feel any unusual side effects or have any difficulties,

discontinue the diet plan immediately and see your doctor.

11. Try to select foods that take a longer time to eat—this will give you the illusion of eating more.

12. Linger longer over your meal by dividing it into as many courses as possible—without exceeding the total amount of food prescribed.

13. At mealtime distract your attention away from food—remember, the more you talk, the less you eat.

SUPER LOW-CALORIE MENUS
TO KEEP YOU IN SHAPE

(Including approximate calorie count based on average restaurant serving)

Jumbo Shrimp Plate
Fresh jumbo shrimp
Lettuce and tomato
Cocktail sauce
  (150 calories)

Fiesta Salad
South African lobster chunks
Lettuce and tomato
Cocktail sauce
  (150 calories)

Office Vitality Booster
Sliced hard-cooked egg
Chopped raw vegetables
Cottage cheese
Lettuce and tomato
  (200 calories)

Easy-do Salad
Half cantaloupe filled with berries
Cottage cheese
  (150 calories)

Health Bowl
Cubed fresh fruit
Cottage cheese
Bed of lettuce
  (250 calories)

Fruit Bowl
Cubed fresh fruit
Sherbet or jello
Bed of lettuce
  (225 calories)

Hawaiian Delight
Pineapple slices
Prunes
Cottage cheese
Bed of lettuce
(*275 calories*)

Spring Salad
Cottage cheese
Chopped fresh garden vegetables
Sour cream garni
(*175 calories*)

Mix-and-Match Salad
Grapefruit and orange wedges
Cottage cheese
Bed of lettuce
(*200 calories*)

Take-It-or-Leave-It Salad
Stewed prunes
Canned peaches
Jello
Cottage cheese
Bed of lettuce
(*250 calories*)

Glamour Salad
Diced chicken salad or chopped
liver
Lettuce and tomato
Bacon strips
Melba toast points
(*175 calories*)

Sweetheart Plate
Half cantaloupe filled with diced
fresh fruit
Orange sherbet
Slice date nut bread
(*225 calories*)

Super Chef's Salad
Green salad tossed with sliced
turkey, Virginia ham,
tongue, Swiss cheese, to-
mato and hard-boiled
egg wedges
(*225 calories*)

Junior Chef's Salad
Green salad tossed with sliced
turkey, salami, American
cheese, and tomato
wedges
(*200 calories*)

Fresh Shrimp Bowl
Jumbo shrimp
Lettuce and tomato
Hard-cooked egg wedges
Cocktail sauce
(*175 calories*)

Lobster Bowl
South African lobster chunks
Tossed salad greens
Tomato and hard-cooked egg
wedges
(*175 calories*)

11

The Office Party Cook-in

Planning an office party is fun. It is also a good way to gain experience for the time when you have a party or entertain your friends at home. The following tips should guarantee you a smashing success:

- Plan a food theme—Chinese food, Italian food, hot dishes, cold buffet, festive, or whatever pleases the majority.
- Schedule a starting and ending time for the party. This way you know how much food to buy for the length of time involved—because when the food's gone, the party's over.
- Arrange for an uncluttered serving area that is equipped with electrical outlets and is easily accessible to guests.
- Decorations can be the most rewarding part of your party plan. Be as creative as you wish; food always looks more appetizing when the setting is pretty to look at. A word to the wise: Since this is your office party and you will be responsible for the

mess, make the dishes paper and the silverware plastic. The variety of designs available is endless. The three-in-one divider plates are quite elegant. Purchase hot or cold cups. Most of these items are designed to match or coordinate with each other. A few artificial flowers or colorful centerpieces add to the decoration picture. It is worth the extra money to get that total magazine ad look.

Bright, lilting music in the background gets the mood of the party going. A small portable radio appropriately placed— and not too loud—will create a party feeling.

Everybody can get into the act with the Office Party Cook-in. Since this is a group effort each girl should try to contribute something to prepare the food in the office, or to keep the food at the right temperature. If a chafing dish or heating tray is not available in the office don't go out and buy one: Borrow. Someone is sure to have the item. If the utensil is heated by sterno, candle, or alcohol, remember to have it available at the time of the party. Running out at the last minute to purchase an item should not be necessary.

The following party themes will give you an idea of what to prepare and how to serve. You will soon be thinking of many variations of your own to experiment with, not only at the office but when entertaining at home as well. You may use any of the recipes in this book for your office party; just remember to increase the ingredients to accommodate the number of people who will attend.

Happy partying!

CANAPÉ AND
HORS d'OEUVRE PARTY

Canapés and hors d'oeuvres are appetizers served with beverages. The difference between the two is that canapés are usually served on bread or pastry while hors d'oeuvres are served alone, although they may be accompanied by bread or pastry.

CANAPÉS
Combine white, whole wheat, brown, or rye bread cut into various shapes: wedges, triangles, rectangles, rounds; or use crackers, which are available in many flavors, sizes, and shapes. For spreads use butter, mayonnaise, or spreads that include cheeses, eggs, bacon, or shrimp and other seafoods. Garnish with greens and seasoning.

HORS D'OEUVRES
There are infinite varieties, but the most popular are shrimp, crab, sardines, eggs, cheese, celery, olives, chopped beef, bologna, mushrooms, oysters, and chopped liver.

DIPS
They add flavor and variety to any hors d'oeuvre. Dips may be placed in a bowl or hollowed-out cabbage, grapefruit, or eggplant. Sour cream, cheese, clam, crabmeat, tuna, caviar, mustard, or tomato sauce are among the many variations from which to choose.

The commercially prepared dips or make-it-yourself mixes are a muncher's delight. Plan to serve at least one or two dips at your party. Center the dip in a bowl on a large plate, surrounded with crackers, potato chips, or other "dipping" foods.

Following are some ever popular dip recipes.

Fish 'n' Chip Dip

1 7½-ounce can tuna
½ cup mayonnaise
1 teaspoon prepared mustard

1 teaspoon lemon juice
6 black olives

Drain and flake tuna; put in a bowl and stir in remaining ingredients, except olives. Mix well and top with olives. Place dip in center of a round tray and surround with plain and seasoned potato chips. If desired serve with more black olives in a small bowl on the side, with toothpicks for dipping. *Makes 1 cup.*

Onion Dip

1 1⅜-ounce envelope onion soup
   mix

1 pint sour cream

Blend mix thoroughly with sour cream. Chill. Serve with potato chips. *Makes 2 cups.*

Cottage Cheese Dip

1 8-ounce container cottage cheese
1 teaspoon dill dip mix

1 tablespoon parsley flakes
1 teaspoon onion flakes

Beat together cottage cheese and dip mix. Stir in parsley and onion flakes. Mix thoroughly and chill until served. *Makes 1½ cups.*

Cheese-Bacon Dip

2 6-ounce packages cream cheese
1½ tablespoons mayonnaise
1 tablespoon cream

3 tablespoons bacon chips or 5
 slices bacon, crumbled
1 teaspoon onion flakes

Mix all ingredients and beat until smooth. Chill. *Makes 1½ cups.*

COMPLETE PARTY MENUS

Cold Platter Party

Sliced roast beef
Potato salad
Sliced baked ham
Coleslaw
Salami
Rye bread
Chocolate layer cake
Coffee

Serving Arrangement

Arrange all foods on a large platter with parsley flakes separating each food. Have tongs or forks available for easy pick-up. Since this is a sandwich-and-side-dish-type party, be sure that you have mustard, mayonnaise, and other relishes available.

The All-Occasion Party #1

Cream cheese and anchovy canapés
Tuna and Rice with Mushrooms*
Garlic sticks
Buns
Fruit tarts
Beverage

* See recipe page 66.

Serving Arrangement

While tuna and rice recipe is being prepared, serve canapés. Serve the entrée from a chafing dish. Arrange open buns on serving plates and pour tuna and rice mixture onto them.

The All-Occasion Party #2

Egg Squares*
Fish 'n' Chip Dip*
Fried Scallops in Newburg Sauce*
Pound cake with chocolate sauce
Beverage

* See recipes pages 60, 132, and 66.

Serving Arrangement

Serve Egg Squares on a serving tray. Place Fish 'n' Chip Dip in the center of a round tray, surrounded by plain and seasoned potato chips. Fried Scallops in Newburg Sauce should be served from a chafing dish with toothpicks for dipping. Place pound cake slices on individual plates and spoon on chocolate sauce (directly from can, if canned sauce is used).

Fondue Party

Swiss Cheese Fondue*
Frankfurter chunks
Baby tomatoes
Waffle squares
Fruit cake
Beverage

* See recipe page 63.

Serving Arrangement

Thaw frozen waffles and cut into 2-inch squares; arrange on a serving tray with Swiss Cheese Fondue. On a second serving tray place half the frankfurter chunks to the left, tomatoes in the center, and remaining frankfurter chunks to the right. Be sure to have enough fondue forks or the equivalent on hand so that guests can dip waffle squares and frankfurter chunks into the fondue.

Italian-style Office Party

Pizza Bits*
Spicy Meatballs*
Mini Spaghetti with Cheese Sauce*
Italian bread
Apple crumb cake
Beverage

* See recipes pages 62, 79, and 61.

Serving Arrangement

Prepare Spicy Meatballs and Mini Spaghetti with Cheese Sauce at home. Serve Pizza Bits on a heating tray. Use one chafing dish each for the spaghetti and the meatballs.

Chinese-style Office Party

Shrimp egg rolls with sweet and sour sauce
Chinatown Chicken*
Beef Fried Rice with Nuts*
Chow mein noodles
Fortune cookies
Pineapple chunks
Beverage

* See recipes pages 80 and 103.

Serving Arrangement

Prepare Chinatown Chicken at home; serve it cold in the office. On a heating tray set at 250°, place dishes of Beef Fried Rice and shrimp egg rolls to keep hot while serving: set sweet and sour sauce to one side. Put chicken in a large serving dish and noodles in a small one. Drain juice from pineapple chunks and place chunks in center of a paper plate; insert a toothpick into each chunk. Surround chunks with fortune cookies and serve.

Christmas or New Year's Party

Chicken Apple Squares*
Potato chips and crackers
Cheese-Bacon Dip*
Pretty Baby Franks*
Ham and cucumber canapes
French pastry
Beverage

* See recipes pages 81, 133, and 79.

Serving Arrangement

On a large serving dish place Chicken Apple Squares to the left, Pretty Baby Franks in the center, and ham and cucumber canapés to the right: keep warm on a heating tray. Put potato chips in a large bowl. Arrange crackers around Cheese-Bacon Dip. Arrange French pastry on a decorative paper serving plate.

COFFEE FOR A CROWD

Bring an electric percolator to the office for your coffee time. (Borrow one for the occasion if you don't have your own.) Since coffee is usually served at the end of a gathering or party it should have an elegant air to provide a festive finishing touch. The coffee can be made in advance and kept hot until served. Allow at least two cups for each person. If the percolator holds less than the required amount, simply pour the extra coffee into another pot and keep hot until needed.

Use regular or all-purpose grind when making coffee in an electric percolator. Follow manufacturer's instructions carefully. Be sure that the inside container for holding coffee grounds is spotless. Always start with fresh cold water. Remember to remove the basket when coffee is finished perking. The percolator can be kept plugged in to keep the coffee hot without further cooking. (When finished serving, however, remember to unplug it.)

Freeze-dried or instant coffee can also be used. Again, follow manufacturer's instructions for best results.

12

Home and Office Food Storage

NONREFRIGERATED STORAGE

CANNED FOODS
Store in as cool a place as possible; the higher the temperature the more rapidly most canned goods lose flavor, color, and nutritive value. Freezing is not recommended since the contents may swell and break the seam of the can. Canned food that has accidentally frozen, however, is safe to use if the can is not damaged.

After canned foods have been opened, any leftovers may be covered and stored in the original can in the refrigerator. High-acid-content foods, such as citrus fruits, may develop a metallic taste when stored as leftovers in their original metal cans; but this will not make them unsafe to eat.

CONDIMENTS
Mustard, relishes, catsup, and chili sauce can usually be stored

at room temperature, but check the label to be sure; once opened, they may lose their flavor and color if stored for long periods in a warm place.

JAMS, JELLIES, AND SYRUPS
Most of these keep well at room temperature even after opened, provided that the storage period is short; the high-sugar content discourages yeast and bacterial growth. Chocolate and table syrups, however, may need refrigeration, especially in warm weather.

SHORTENINGS AND SALAD OILS
Most oils and shortenings can be stored at room temperature. They have either a natural antioxidant or an antioxidant added to them; this agent helps keep the fats from developing a rancid flavor caused by exposure to oxygen. Many oils are also protected by storing them in a dark bottle that prevents light from entering. Butter or margarine, of course, must always be kept refrigerated.

BREADSTUFFS AND BAKED GOODS
Keep cereal and cracker boxes as tightly closed as possible to protect contents from moisture; otherwise, they will lose their crispness. Remember, too, that even the best housekeepers sometimes discover weevils or other insects in flour and cereals stored on cupboard shelves. Metal, glass, or plastic containers with tight-fitting lids will help control insects as well as protect the food from moisture. Cover baked foods to prevent excessive drying and store in a clean and dry place to discourage mold growth.

DAIRY PRODUCTS
Grated hard cheese in a covered container keeps well at room temperature, but most others should be kept refrigerated. All cheeses, except soft, unripened types, taste best if taken from the refrigerator and kept at room temperature about an hour before serving.

Milk and cream, of course, should always be kept chilled. Store dry milk in a cool, dry place, but never for too long; off-flavors and off-odors can develop after a certain amount of time.

Fresh Produce

Potatoes, onions, winter squash, and apples keep well in a cool, dry place. Remove them from their unventilated paper bags because circulation of air helps prevent mold and decay. Store tomatoes and most fruits at room temperature if they require additional ripening, but do not place them in direct sunlight.

REFRIGERATION

Fresh Meat and Poultry

Prepackaged meat from the supermarket may be stored in original wrapper if the meat is to be used within one or two days; if not, loosen the wrapper so that air may dry the surface of the meat. Also loosen or remove the wrapping if the meat has been cut to order and packaged in market wrapping paper. Loosen wrappings on poultry to allow circulation of air. For best results, use poultry and ground meats within two days; roasts, chops, and steaks three to five days.

Dairy Products

Keep milk and cream covered to prevent bacterial growth and protect flavor. If possible, try to keep storage place dark, as exposure to light can harm flavors and destroy riboflavin and other important nutritive elements of milk.

Hard and semi-hard cheeses, wrapped tightly to prevent drying, will keep for many weeks. Mold is not necessarily harmful; if it appears remove it and use the rest of the cheese. Store aromatic cheeses in covered containers. Cheese spreads, once opened, should be tightly covered. Unripened cheeses, such as cottage and cream cheese, should be covered and stored for only a few days.

FROZEN FOODS

If the temperature in your frozen food storage compartment is between 15° to 20° F, keep foods there only one or two weeks.

FRESH PRODUCE

Store leafy vegetables, broccoli, and cauliflower in plastic bags or in the refrigerator crisper to prevent evaporation and wilting. To "crisp" vegetables wash and drain them before refrigerating. Store lettuce in a bag by itself to control rust colored spotting that increases on contact with other vegetables. Store fruits whole and uncovered. Store berries unwashed, in a shallow container.

FREEZER TIPS

Remove original wrapping from packaged fresh meat and poultry. The paper may not be moisture- and air-resistant and may impart unpleasant flavors to the meat; also, the cardboard plate absorbs moisture and may stick to the meat during thawing. Be sure poultry pieces are clean; package giblets separately. Wrap meat or poultry in nonporous freezer paper and freeze immediately. For best results and practical freezer management, use within two or three months.

Homogenized milk can be frozen satisfactorily. If purchased in paper cartons, freeze milk in the original carton; if purchased in glass bottles, allow some air space for expansion during freezing. Heavy cream may also be frozen, but its whipping quality will be impaired.

Cheese can be frozen without harm to flavor, and freezing will help prevent mold development. However, freezing causes texture changes in most cheeses, making them crumbly and hard to slice. Wrap them in freezer paper before freezing.

Store frozen foods immediately and keep at 0° F or below until ready to use.

Freezing is not recommended for salad-type vegetables, such as lettuce, celery, and tomatoes. These vegetables have a high water content and freezing causes undesirable texture changes.

Many baked goods can be frozen—some more successfully than others—so experiment with freezing your favorite kinds. Freezing is not recommended, however, for cream fillings, soft meringues, and certain frostings. Because freezing does not freshen stale foods, start with freshly baked goods. For best results wrap in freezer paper and use in one to two months.

The following list shows how long certain foods can be stored in the freezer (at 0°):

Beef, lamb, veal	9 to 12 months
Beef (ground)	3 to 4 months
Poultry, fish	4 months
Bread	3 to 4 months
Cakes	3 to 4 months
Cooked casseroles	2 to 3 months
Soups	3 months
Sandwiches	2 to 3 weeks
Leftover cooked foods	2 to 3 weeks
Hors d'oeuvres	2 months

Some foods don't belong in the freezer at all, for example, salad greens and other salad ingredients (peppers, celery, cucumbers, onions, tomatoes). Cream separates during freezing and hard cheeses tend to crumble. Mayonnaise, salad dressings, and cooked egg mixtures should not be frozen. Cooked meats which have been frozen can be frozen again. However, other cooked foods, such as vegetables, stews, and casseroles, which have been frozen should not be refrozen once completely thawed.

Appendix

A. CALORIE CHART

MEATS AND
POULTRY   *Calories*
Bacon (fried crisp), 2 slices   95
Beef tongue, 3 ounces   205
Bologna, 1 slice, 4-inch
  diam.   85
Chicken (broiled), 3
  ounces   180
Frankfurter, 1 medium   155
Ham (canned), 2 ounces   170
Ham (smoked), 3 ounces   290
Ham (smoked), 1 cup,
  diced   320
Hamburger (lean,
  broiled), 4 ounces   245
Lamb chop (lean,
  broiled), 2.5 ounces   140
Leg of lamb, 2.5 ounces   130
Pot pie, 8 ounces   460

Roast beef (lean),
  4 ounces   210
Roast pork (lean),
  2.5 ounces   175
Roast veal (lean),
  3 ounces   280
Sausage, 4 ounces   340
Steak (lean, broiled),
  4 ounces   235
Turkey, drumstick and
  thigh with bone
  (fried), 5 ounces   275
Veal cutlet (broiled),
  3 ounces   185

FISH AND
SHELLFISH
Bluefish (baked or
  broiled), 3 ounces   135

FISH AND
SHELLFISH (cont.)   *Calories*
Clam, 1 medium   9
Crabmeat, 3 ounces   90
Haddock (fried),
  3 ounces   135
Mackerel (broiled),
  3 ounces   200
Oyster, 1 medium   12
Salmon (canned), 3 ounces   120
Sardines (canned),
  3 ounces   180
Shad (baked), 3 ounces   170
Shrimp, 1 medium   10
Swordfish (broiled, with
  butter), 3 ounces   150
Tuna (canned), 3 ounces   170

VEGETABLES

Asparagus, 1 medium spear   3-5
Avocado, 1 medium, half   185
Baked beans (canned),
  1 cup   320
Beets, 1 cup   70
Broccoli, 1 cup   45
Brussels sprouts, 1 cup   60
Cabbage (cooked), 1 cup,
  shredded   45
Cabbage (raw), 1 cup,
  shredded   25
Carrots (cooked), 1 cup,
  diced   45
Carrots (raw), 1 medium,
  5½ inches long   20
Cauliflower (cooked),
  1 cup   30
Celery, 1 stalk, 8 inches
  long   5
Corn (canned), 1 cup   170

Corn (cooked), 1 ear,
  5 inches long   65
Cucumber, 1 medium,
  7½ inches long   25
Lettuce, 1 head, 5-inch
  diam.   70
Lettuce, 2 large leaves   5
Lima beans, 1 cup   150
Mushrooms, 1 cup   30
Onions (cooked), 1 cup   80
Onion (raw), 1 medium,
  2½-inch diam.   50
Parsley (raw), 1 table-
  spoon, chopped   1
Peas (canned or frozen),
  1 cup   80
Peas (fresh, cooked),
  1 cup   110
Potato (baked, with
  peel), 1 medium   105
Potato (baked, without peel),
  1 medium   90
Potato (boiled), 1 medium   90
Potato (French-fried),
  1 piece   15
Potato (mashed, with milk,
  no butter), 1 cup   145
Radish (raw), 1 medium   3
Sauerkraut, 1 cup   30
Spinach, 1 cup   45
String beans, 1 cup   35
Summer squash, 1 cup   35
Sweet potato (baked),
  1 medium   155
Sweet potato (candied),
  1 medium   295
Tomato (canned), 1 cup   45
Tomato (raw), 1 medium   30
Tomato juice, 1 cup   50
Winter squash, 1 cup   95

FRUITS

	Calories
Apple, 1 medium	70
Apple juice, 1 cup	125
Applesauce (canned, sweetened), 1 cup	185
Apricots (canned, with syrup), 1 cup	220
Apricot (fresh), 1 medium	20
Banana, 1 medium	85
Blackberries, 1 cup	85
Blueberries, 1 cup	85
Cantaloupe, 1 medium, 5-inch diam., half	40
Cherries, 1 cup	65
Cranberry sauce (canned), 1 cup	550
Dates (pitted), 1 cup	505
Fig (dried), 1 large	60
Fruit cocktail (canned, in syrup), 1 cup	195
Grapefruit, 1 medium, 5-inch diam., half	55
Grapefruit juice (fresh), 1 cup	95
Grapes, 1 cup	85
Grape juice (bottled), 1 cup	165
Lemon, 1 medium	20
Orange, 1 medium	65
Orange juice, (fresh), 1 cup	110
Peach (fresh), 1 medium, 2-inch diam.	35
Peaches (canned, in syrup, pitted), 1 cup	200
Pear, 1 medium, 3-inch diam.	100
Pineapple (fresh), 1 cup, diced	75
Pineapple (canned, in syrup), 1 cup	205
Plum, 1 medium, 2-inch diam.	30
Prune (cooked, unsweetened), 1 medium	17
Prune juice (canned), 1 cup	170
Raisins, 1 cup	460
Raisins, 1 tablespoon	30
Strawberries (fresh), 1 cup	70
Tangerine, 1 medium, 2½-inch diam.	40
Watermelon, 1 wedge, 4" × 8"	120

DAIRY PRODUCTS

American cheese, 1 cube, 1" × 1"	70
American cheese, 1 slice	105
Butter, 1 cup or 2 sticks	1,605
Butter, 1 pat	50
Buttermilk, 1 cup	90
Cottage cheese (creamed), 1 ounce	30
Cream (light), 1 cup	525
Cream (light), 1 tablespoon	35
Cream (heavy), 1 tablespoon	50
Cream cheese, 1 ounce	105
Egg (hard-cooked), 1 large	80
Egg (scrambled, with butter), 1 large	115
Egg white (raw), 1 large	20
Egg yolk (raw), 1 large	60
Farmer cheese, 1 ounce	25
Margarine, 1 cup or 2 sticks	1,615
Margarine, 1 pat	50
Milk (skim), 1 cup	90
Milk (whole), 1 cup	165
Pot cheese, 1 ounce	25
Roquefort cheese, 1 ounce	105
Swiss cheese, 1 ounce	105
Yogurt (plain), 1 cup	120

BREADSTUFFS

	Calories
Bread (plain or toasted), 1 medium slice	60
Cereal (cooked), 1 cup	105
Cereal (dry, unsweetened), 1 average serving	110
Graham cracker, 1 medium	28
Macaroni (cooked), 1 cup	155
Muffin, 1 medium, 3-inch diam.	140
Noodles (cooked), 1 cup	200
Pancake, 1 medium, 4-inch diam.	55
Rice (cooked), 1 cup	200
Roll, 1 medium	130
Rye wafer, 1 wafer	25
Saltine, 1 square	23
Spaghetti (cooked), 1 cup	155
Waffle, 1 medium	240

SWEETS

Angel food cake, 1 piece, 2 inches wide	110
Caramel, 1 medium	40
Chocolate bar (milk or dark), 1 small	145
Chocolate layer cake, 1 piece, 2 inches wide	420
Chocolate syrup, 1 tablespoon	20
Cookie, 1 average, 3-inch diam.	110
Doughnut (plain), 1 medium	135
Fig bar, 1 small	55
Fudge, 1 medium piece	120
Gelatin, ½ cup	80
Gelatin (sugar-free), ½ cup	10
Honey, 1 tablespoon	60
Ice cream, ½ cup	200

Ice cream soda, 1 average	350
Ice milk, 1 cup	285
Ices, ½ cup	120
Jams, jellies, preserves, 1 tablespoon	55
Lemon meringue pie, 1 piece, 4-inch diam.	300
Pie (fruit), 1 piece, 4 inches wide	330
Pound cake, 1 piece, 3″ × 2″ × 1½″	180
Pudding, custard, 1 cup	275
Sherbet, ½ cup	120
Sponge cake, 1 piece, 2 inches wide	115
Sugar (granulated), 1 cup	770
Sugar (granulated), 1 teaspoon	16
Syrup, 1 tablespoon	55

MISCELLANEOUS

Alcoholic beverages, ⅛ cup	75
Beer, 1 cup	110
Carbonated beverages (general), 1 cup	80
Catsup, 1 tablespoon	15
Chili sauce, 1 tablespoon	15
Cocktail, 1 average	150
Cocoa, 1 cup	235
Coffee (black), 1 cup	0
Cola, 1 cup	105
Cooking oil, 1 tablespoon	125
Cornstarch, 1 cup	275
French dressing, 1 tablespoon	125
Ginger ale, 1 cup	80
Mayonnaise, 1 tablespoon	110
Nuts (shelled), ½ cup	375
Olives (green), 1 large	9

Peanut butter, 1 tablespoon 90	Russian dressing, 1 tablespoon 75
Peanuts (roasted, shelled),	Soup (clear, vegetable), 1 cup 80
½ cup 420	Soup (creamed), 1 cup 200
Pickles (dill or sweet), 1 large 18	Soup (rice, noodle, barley),
Pizza (cheese), 1 medium	1 cup 115
slice 200	Tea (black), 1 cup 1
Potato chips, 1 medium 11	

B. FREEZE-DRIED FOODS

(Serves 4)

COMPLETE MEALS	PRICE*
Applesauce, pancake mix, maple syrup mix, sweet milk cocoa, no-stick cooking oil	$2.10
Orange juice drink, eggs, bacon bits, hashed brown potatoes, sweet milk cocoa, no-stick cooking oil	2.87
Applesauce, scrambled eggs with ham, hashed brown potatoes, sweet milk cocoa, no-stick cooking oil	3.80
Swiss cheese with "bac-o-crisps," melba toast, beef jerky, fruit punch	2.80
Spicy apple chips, grape jelly spread, peanut butter spread, pilot biscuits, vanilla shake mix	2.73
Corned beef, blackberry jelly spread, pilot biscuits, chocolate shake mix	2.80
Chopped beef, cheddar cheese spread, pilot biscuits, strawberry shake mix	3.17
White meat tuna salad spread, pilot biscuits, lemon-lime fruit drink, trail snack	3.40
Chicken à la king, corn, mashed potatoes, vanilla pudding, orange beverage	3.53

* Prices may vary in different parts of the country.

Vegetable beef soup, chicken-rice dinner, French apple compote,
lemon beverage   3.48

French onion soup, beef stroganoff with noodles, banana cream
pudding, grape beverage   3.68

BEEF COURSES
Beef Stroganoff with Noodles	2.32
Spaghetti with Meatballs	2.25

CHICKEN COURSES
Chicken Romanoff	2.32
Savory Chicken Pilaf	2.25
Chicken-Rice	1.98
Chicken à la King	1.63

HAM COURSES
Ham 'n' Beans	2.10
Ham and Cheese	2.00

MEATS
Meatballs	1.18
Beef	1.20
Chicken	1.25
Ham	1.42
Corned Beef	1.58
Ground Beef	1.00
Diced Chicken	.90

SPECIALTY DINNERS
Corned Beef Skillet	2.32
Shrimp Creole	2.57
Fiesta Mexicana Dinner	1.53

Turkey Supreme with Noodles	2.17
Macaroni and Cheese	1.00
Spanish Rice Dinner	1.00
Beef Taco Comida	1.92
Vegetable Beef Stew	2.22
Chili Mac with Beef	1.92
Western Hash	1.92
Chili Con Carne Ranchero	2.03

SHAKE MIXES

Chocolate	.60
Strawberry	.60
Vanilla	.60
Sweet Milk Cocoa	.47
Instant Milk Blend	.40

SPREADS

White Meat Tuna Salad	1.75
Cheddar Cheese	.70
Swiss Cheese with Bac-O-Crisps	.70
Crunchy Peanut Butter	.50
Blackberry Jelly	.30
Grape Jelly	.30

DESSERTS

No-Bake Pineapple Cheese Cake with Graham Cracker Crust	.80
No-Bake Fudge Brownie Mix with Walnuts	.75
French Apple Compote	.60
Wild Cherry Gel-Dessert	.40
Chocolate Pudding	.55
Vanilla Pudding	.45
Butterscotch Pudding	.45
Banana Cream Pudding	.55
Lemon Pudding	.45
Toasted Coconut Pudding	.45

INDEX